Did You Know We Had a Screen Door?

Claire Laishley

Did You Know
We Had a Screen Door?

This book is for
the man in my life
(and the life in my man)
Garry

Did You Know We Had a Screen Door?
ISBN 978 1 74027 562 0
Copyright © text Claire Laishley 2009
Cover illustration by Geoff Reynolds

First published 2009
Reprinted 2015

GINNINDERRA PRESS
PO Box 3461 Port Adelaide 5015
www.ginninderrapress.com.au

1

'That's something I've always wanted to do!'

It seemed everyone we spoke to shared the dream – to travel around the countryside in a motorhome. And although there has always been a large population of highway patrollers, with the threat of terrorism around the world, more Australians are choosing to holiday on their own soil.

But I couldn't help wondering. If everyone who made this statement actually followed through on their dream, the traffic jam generated would create so much road rage, Australia would soon be facing its own form of terrorism. Unlike these adventurous souls, however, this was one dream I had never shared. Road trips were not part of the happy memories of my youth, and the three I did participate in were disastrous.

The first, when I was eight years old, was to a popular beachside suburb of Adelaide called Glenelg. Although it was only thirteen kilometres from our house in St Peters, this did not deter my parents from packing the entire contents of the house, and soon the family's British racing green Austin A40 was sitting closer to the ground than originally designed. As it took several hours to travel those few kilometres, it's safe to say my father did not let the colour choice influence his driving style. But this particular holiday nearly didn't happen.

Three days before we were due to set off, I looked in the mirror and burst into tears. My entire body was covered with the unmistakable signs of chickenpox. A family conference was called regarding the pending vacation, and my mother declared it less than responsible to take a child away who was so obviously unwell. My father was playing it down, not through any lack of concern for his darling daughter, I hasten to add, but more from watching his annual leave dissolve into red spots. Both parents were intractable, and the only thing they could agree on was that the final decision should rest with someone who held the appropriate authority.

Our local general practitioner was a humourless sort and, as I sat on the examination table, he peered at me through a round eyepiece attached to a leather band strapped round his head, and threw a glance in my mother's direction. 'It's chickenpox. Make sure she doesn't scratch, otherwise she'll be scarred for life!' he said, and then dismissed us.

'Yes, but is it safe to take her on holidays to Glenelg?' said my mother, playing the immovable object she could become when pushed.

'Glenelg's no different from anywhere else,' he replied, and so we would not mistake his intentions again, opened the door and pointed to the waiting room.

Not quite the guidance my mother was seeking, but assuming geographical location would not affect the 'scratch factor', and reluctant to disappoint my older brother, who was ready to commit sororicide, therefore eliminating the impediment to his happy holiday, she advised the males of the house that everything was go.

Being an extremely well organised and meticulous man, my father had phoned the guest house owner several times leading up to the holiday to confirm different points about the accommodation. After each call, Dad would enthuse so much that, by the time we were due to leave home, we couldn't wait for that first glimpse of our luxurious beach-side abode.

My father had requested an upper-level apartment with a view, but our collective hearts hit rock bottom when he pulled up outside a tired two-storey weatherboard built around the 1920s and untouched by human hands or paintbrush since. My mother's silence spoke volumes as we lugged the household contents up the rickety staircase which clung with desperation to the side of the building.

The 'apartment' comprised two minuscule bedrooms, a bathroom the size of an ironing-board cupboard and a lounge area with hot plates, sink and a fridge in the corner. Every room was painted lettuce green with touches of pale butter yellow, and if you wanted even a glimpse of the ocean you had to drag a chair up to the window and, while standing on it, lean precariously to the right.

And to top off a disastrous start to the holiday, my brother and I were horrified to realise we would be sharing the second bedroom.

"You can take the top bunk, dear,' my mother said, pointing at me. 'That way your germs will stay around the ceiling and not infect your brother.'

It was obvious from the thunderous look on my brother's face that he was less than pleased with this arrangement, and Mum was quick to notice.

'Oh well, Christopher, if you catch it as well, that's the end of any trips across the road to the amusement park.'

I could never understand why it was necessary to share this piece of information with me as well.

And so holiday hell began! Each day I would lie, imprisoned in the top bunk by the wicked witch, listening to the squeals of delight from the Ferris wheel across the road. It was safe to say that my green complexion had little to do with any medical condition or, in fact, the colour of the walls.

I was recalling this trip with my brother recently and took the opportunity to remind him once again that he had been the favoured child.

'Yeah, so favoured I had to go to the local primary school for the entire two weeks we were on holidays,' he said.

I opened my mouth to object, but suddenly a vague memory started to take shape. I remembered him walking into the bedroom one afternoon with a bloodied lip and the false boyhood bravado which often masked humiliation. It had been pointed out to him that you didn't just show up at a new school and expect to be one of the gang straight away.

'But at least you went on the rides after school each day,' I said, determined not to let the sympathy vote drift too far from me.

Each parent took turns to accompany him to the sideshows after school, so he had a chance to spend his pocket money, and it did nothing for sibling affection when he came back brandishing prizes he'd won for shooting at moving ducks.

'I'm pretty good at this,' he announced one afternoon. 'I could even win you something, if you give me your pocket money.'

The promise of a kewpie doll in a pink tulle skirt made me almost weak at the knees, so without hesitation, I handed over my meagre fortune. Well, I was very young, and he was my big brother. Plus he gave the worst Chinese burns! But strangely enough, when he played for me his aim wasn't too good, so the ducks lived another day and I didn't get my kewpie doll. Well, that's not entirely true. I did buy one at the Royal Show a few years later, but by then their dresses were made of lime green fabric, and it just wasn't the same.

It was a miserable holiday, and the smell of calamine lotion and the feel of woollen mittens still make me scratch. It had been the longest two weeks of my entire life.

The second road trip was far more daring. Dad had been so pleased with the performance of the Austin's maiden marathon journey, he decided to venture further this time. Melbourne was the destination, and while the car was packed to capacity once again, this time there was one extra addition. A hessian water bag with a small plastic stopper was hung from the front grille of the car. At first I thought this might have been refreshment for the trip – that we would stop the car every time someone was thirsty – but it turned out to be spare water for the radiator.

Our liquid needs were kept in two large Woodroofe lemonade bottles on the floor, and were strictly supervised by my mother. Unfortunately, the contents had been consumed months ago and these bottles now held a slightly tinted fluid she optimistically called cordial. Drinks were only allowed at timed intervals, as Dad had meticulously planned how many toilet stops would be necessary. But in the end I was more than happy to remain thirsty, as each toilet stop became an excruciating embarrassment.

My father would dramatically clear his throat, announce, 'Relief stop coming up, everyone,' and, flicking the small yellow indicator out from the left-hand side of the car, pull to a grinding halt a full seven minutes later. My mother would exit the car, stand in full view of the roadside and brandish an enormously large toilet roll. (Thinking back, it probably wasn't any bigger than the standard issue of tissue, but being an age where I was agonisingly self-consciousness about bodily functions – well, about anything, really – the said toilet roll seemed to glow with blinding neon signage.) And just as we were handed our four pieces of Sorbent and directed towards a sparsely foliaged bush, this always seemed to coincide with a passing car filled with laughing, pointing children of my age and older.

As this was the first long trip the Austin had been subjected to, Dad was reluctant to place any undue stress on the vehicle, so the speedometer never passed thirty miles per hour (fifty kmh). To relieve the boredom of the forty days and forty nights it seemed to take to get to the Victorian capital, my mother kept us busy with a variety of games.

'I spy, with my little eye, something starting with SB,' she announced.

Our attention had started to wander after a hundred single-letter objects and, with my score desperately needing a win, I frowned with concentration.

'Sister's bum!' my brother yelled, collapsing with hysteria at his own wit.

My mother's icy stare could have razed an apartment block, and although I would have endured sharp needles slid under my fingernails before admitting it, my brother's answer appealed to me much more than the correct answer of 'spiky bush'.

This fever pitch of excitement took its toll and we started yawning, but my father was well prepared. He had designed sleeping arrangements for both children, and once again the favoured child hit the jackpot. My brother merely stretched out on the padded upholstery of the back seat and slept like a baby. My sleeping area was another story. There was a hump in the middle of the car floor at the back, and Dad had placed a plank of wood across the hump, so at least my makeshift bed was level. But as a handyman, my father was a great dancer, so he'd forgotten to support the plank at either end. I was soon involved in a delicate balancing act as the board became a seesaw, banging down one end and then the other, and with my head close to the wheels, I turned green with motion sickness.

We eventually arrived in Melbourne, had a nice holiday, I suppose, and headed back on the long day's journey into night. I can't really remember too many details. But one thing which is embedded firmly in my memory is hearing my mother's statement when my father suggested another road trip the following year.

'I don't really think road trips agree with Claire. The dear kid seems to get sick every time we go away.'

2

And so I managed to avoid any more holidays involving car travel – until the mid-1960s. The family had moved to Melbourne a few years earlier, and after spending several unremarkable years at secondary school, I decided to join the workforce. I was not only mistress of my own fate, but now I had my own money to spread around the boutiques, fashion houses and music stores of the city. This worked well for twelve months, but then my annual leave came due, and the bank account was showing not only a lack of funds but a lack of interest as well.

My best friend, Lyn, had organised holidays for the same period, but as she was also in the same predicament, our options were severely limited. After long discussions over numerous travel brochures, we came to a decision. The only holiday within our price range was a week in a bed and breakfast at Bright. This is a small township situated in the Ovens Valley, not far from Mt Hotham and Falls Creek, and is popular with the snow skiing crowd. It only became affordable to us because our holidays were in the middle of summer!

Apart from a couple of church camps in my early teens, this was my first holiday without parents, and I couldn't wait. But while we had just enough money to cover accommodation and food, we had forgotten to allow for transport costs. When I dropped this piece of information over the dinner table one night, Dad nearly hyperventilated with excitement.

'It's all right. Your mother and I will drive you there and back.'

Suddenly those childhood holidays flooded back and the warning signs flashed. I was about to refuse when I realised this was a gesture for his sake as well as mine. My father's quick response showed the poor man had been suffering withdrawal symptoms from only driving round the suburbs for the last few years. And at least the Austin had been replaced by a '63 EJ Holden, one of the more conservative designs from the General Motors stable.

'That'd be great, Dad,' I said, hoping he'd located third gear by now.

There was still one slight reservation. We did only have one week's leave, and I couldn't help wondering if there would be time to see much of Bright before making the return journey. One more review of our finances, however, and we soon reached the obvious conclusion – there was no alternative.

A few weeks later, Lyn and I threw our crammed suitcases into the boot of the EJ, and joined the family poodle, Souffee, in the back seat. Our pampered pooch didn't usually come with us in the car, but as my parents were doing the trip there and back in one day, my mother felt it unfair to leave him alone for such a long time.

I had warned Lyn about my father's penchant for 'appreciating the scenery', but after clearing the suburbs, I was amazed to find we were travelling at a fairly respectable speed. The landscape 'whizzed' instead of 'wandered' past and I felt myself relaxing.

But not all the travellers were happy. While initially thrilled to be part of any family activity, our canine friend was anything but relaxed. He appeared to have springs attached to each paw and leapt from the back seat into Mum's lap in the front, let out a howl, and bounced into the back seat once again.

'I think he wants to do woozies, dear,' my mother announced, glancing at my father. 'Quick, pull over.'

I have to say that her expressions were rather unique (all right, embarrassing) but none more so than those relating to bodily functions. As soon as the car stopped, mother and dog hopped out.

'Woooozies!' she trilled, watching the fluff ball disappear into a clump of bushes.

Minutes passed and the silence was deafening.

'Sooooo – feeeee.'

We waited, imagining the large 'poodle puddle' being created, but as the minutes ticked by there was still no sign of 'le chien'.

My mother walked back to the car and stuck her head through my open window. 'This is all your fault, young lady. Now go and find him, and make it quick.'

I failed to see how I could be held responsible for a canine bladder, but anxious to get this show on the road, I got out of the car. But just as I headed for the clump of bushes, Souffee suddenly appeared and, from the colour of his coat, it was obvious he had found the only mud in the area.

'For heaven's sake, that's all we need,' Mum said, shaking her head. Reaching into the glovebox she produced a roll of toilet paper (yes, some things never change) and tossed it in my direction. 'Neither of you are to set foot in the car until that animal is restored to its natural colour.'

I glanced down at my carefully selected travelling outfit of pastel pink and white checked Bermuda shorts and pink crocheted top, and groaned. My entrance into the holiday resort of Bright would be memorable for all the wrong reasons. Twenty minutes later, our poodle was clean and white once again; I couldn't say the same for myself.

We assumed Souffee had taken advantage of the toilet break while investigating the countryside, so were dismayed when he resumed his frenetic activity soon after heading off again. Boing – into the front seat! Boing – into the back seat! Dad was not a confident driver at the best of times (even the radio proved a distraction!) so an airborne hound hurtling round the cabin of the car was an accident waiting to happen. But suddenly Souffee landed on the back seat, let out a plaintive whine and vomited in my lap.

My father's reaction was the quickest I had witnessed in his entire motoring history. As he pulled over to the side of the road, everyone vacated the car in record time – except me. I was left with a sorry-looking dog and an even sorrier-looking outfit. In record time the toilet paper was reduced to a cardboard roll and, thanks to four open windows for the rest of the trip, my Cilla Black bob morphed into a Jackson Five Afro.

Lyn and I did have a wonderful week in Bright, lying by the pool and turning a brilliant red instead of the nut brown we were hoping for, but the thought of the return trip hovered like an ominous cloud. So it was with much relief that I noted the absence of wildlife in the car a week later, when the EJ pulled into the car park.

Soon after this, I started work with an airline company and holidays took on a whole new meaning. With the concessions given to travel industry personnel, I was able to fly to England for my annual leave, paying only ten per cent of the fare. Although I eventually left the airline, I was hooked on the high life, and only chose destinations boasting an airport.

Now all these years later, my darling husband was suggesting we hire a motorhome and hit the highways (and low ways) of Australia for our annual leave. Let the fun begin!

3

The first thing we needed to do for our big road trip was find a big road vehicle and, since I'd accepted this trip was on, I had decided to throw myself into the preparation in a big way. Two months before we were due to leave, I made a list of motorhome dealerships. I figured the sooner I knew how much room I had to play with, the sooner I could organise what to take with us.

On the first available Saturday morning, I threw some toast and tea in my husband's direction, told him he could sleep all day Sunday (I was lying) and waited in the car.

I couldn't believe our luck when the first dealership produced the perfect van. As I stood in the compact kitchen, I could almost smell the sizzling bacon and hear the ping of bread erupting from the toaster.

'This is it – it's perfect,' I said. How easy is this? Yes, it was going to be fun! But HON (Husband of Narrator) wasn't so sure. If he had to be dragged out of a perfectly comfortable bed, he was determined to make a morning of it.

'I don't think we need to decide straight away. We don't know what these others have to offer,' he said, waving the list in my face. I mentally removed the fry pan from the stove and put the bacon back in the fridge.

The next stop was only five minutes down the road, and we were amazed to see not just a few, but rows and rows of luxurious vans all bearing the name Winnebago.

'These are fantastic – we'd really be travelling in style!'

Hon grinned. 'And you would have been quite happy to settle for that inadequate little number up the road?'

'Hi, folks, something I can help you with?'

The silky smooth salesman had been waiting to pounce, but as we started to explain our requirements, he had already produced keys from his back pocket.

'Pretty safe in saying you'll fall in love with this one,' he said, guiding us to the largest van on the lot.

If this salesman had dragged his gaze from my dilated pupils and gaping mouth for a few seconds, he would have realised only half the battle was won.

A statement such as this was like red rag to my Taurean husband. His mouth formed a thin line as his eyes narrowed. 'That remains to be seen,' he muttered.

The van supplied the same sleeping capacity as the one I'd fallen for at the previous dealership, but there the comparison ended. The main area comprised a table and two padded bench seats which could be converted into an extra bed, there was a compact kitchen and a large sofa, and the double bed was suspended above the driving cabin. A bathroom at the end of the van incorporated a shower, bath and toilet, with just enough room for a small vanity. Not only did it have every possible facility, but the décor was tasteful in muted shades of grey, blue and beige. Turning to Hon, I was ready to plead my case, but the salesman was one step ahead.

'I always find once the little woman sees this baby she won't settle for second best.'

I was even prepared to ignore the 'little woman' reference if we could just pick this one, but I needn't have worried. The message my husband was being sent could not have been clearer. If you want the trip to be peaceful, mate, you'll give in now.

I watched the inner turmoil as Hon tried to regain control of the situation, but the fait accompli sign flashed neon, so he mumbled the dates we required the van.

'No worries – free as a bird – and you'll be as well.'

After signing the rental agreement, we walked to the car and I glanced at Hon.

'I'm starting to think that life on the road might be pretty good,' I said. 'I'm glad we didn't settle for the first van. We're going to be travelling the highways of Australia in a five-star hotel.' I was already mentally packing.

And this continued for the next six weeks. It didn't matter how many times I deleted items from the list – and put them back on – I wasn't going to be happy on this trek if we omitted to pack the entire contents of our house. Help – I was turning into my mother!

Finally it was departure day. As soon as the dawn light filtered through the bedroom curtains, I was out of bed; there was so much preparation for our big adventure. But not so the man of the house! Darl (Dreamy and Remarkably Languid) figured that holidays are for sleep-ins, and the alarm had been switched to the off position. But not even he could sleep through my sighs and slamming doors, and wisely decided to welcome the day sooner rather than later.

'I'm off to pick up the van,' he announced an hour later.

This was it. We were about to become the proud temporary owners of a Winnebago campervan. Eat our dust!

An hour later, I was standing outside talking to a neighbour, when I glanced up and saw something resembling a removalist's van turning into the driveway. The Winnebago had arrived!

'Here he is!' I shrieked, and laughed when I saw the grin on Hon's face. My boy had a new toy, and I watched in awe as he manoeuvred this small building down the drive and into the parking space. But then amazement turned to horror when I heard a grating sound.

'Watch out – the garage eaves!' I yelled.

He stepped from the driving cabin, surveyed the mark down the side of the van and nodded. 'Well, at least it gives me some sort of perspective regarding the height of this thing. That'll come in handy for future parking,' he calmly stated.

Was the man an idiot? In the past I had always admired his cool attitude, but not this time. In a matter of seconds, I was already planning how to cancel the holiday and hand over our life savings to cover the damage.

'Oh my God, what are we going to do?' I said, convinced my personal rogue fairy of road trips was wreaking early havoc.

Hon squinted at the side of the van. 'Lucky it's only a surface scratch,' he said, and disappeared into the house. He emerged a few minutes later with a sponge and detergent, and proceeded to eliminate any sign of damage. My hero!

4

There's an official name for it – ataxophobia! That's the fear of disorder or untidiness, and I've had to face the facts – I have attacks of 'atax'. That's the only way I can explain my penchant for lists. Disorder makes me nervous and, in order to keep my life in order, I make lists. I've been doing this all my life. The first list I remember was when I was four years old. Not being a child prodigy and unable to write, this 'things to do' list was etched in my memory, and still is.

> I want to walk to kindergarten at the end of the road without Mum watching.
> I want to take the ankle straps off my party shoes and look like I'm five
> I want to play on the boys' boat in the kindergarten playground.
> I want my hair cut in a fringe.

I even promised Mum I wouldn't ask for another thing for the rest of my life if I could only have a fringe. All those wishes were eventually achieved, even though Mum wasn't too keen on the fringe idea, but that was all right. I saved her a trip to the hairdressers.

And these lists were never more important than when we were planning a holiday. My previous holiday lists had been such simple documents. One suitcase and one list which itemised every piece of clothing I possessed. This was usually enough to send me away well prepared. But I soon found that packing to travel around in a motorhome needed some serious organisation, and the list became impressive for its subheadings alone.

I discovered 'Food Box' was too general. After all, there was 'Fridge Food', 'Dry Food' and 'Breakfast Food', not to mention 'Food for Thought' (chocolate and lollies). And the same applied to the 'Entertainment Box'. This was divided into 'Puzzle Book Box', 'Games Box' and 'Library Box'.

Some people may find this labelling a trifle over the top, but just think about it. After an exhausting day on the road, all you want is a quick meal and a game before you hit the sack. But where did you put the packets of pasta and the deck of cards? Believe me, when the Winnebago wanderlust hits your house, you'll thank me!

One thing we had noticed about 'our gal Winnie' was her enormous amount of storage space. There were cupboards under the bench, above the bench, next to the bed, over the bed, next to the driver's cabin, under the vanity, next to the vanity and even under the floor. I gazed at the sea of boxes I had been filling for the last few weeks, and smiled. It all looked terribly organised, and I was a happy traveller.

But when we loaded the first box into the van, things came unstuck. We quickly discovered that none of the van cupboards were large enough to accommodate a cardboard box! So after weeks of hard work, there was no alternative. We unpacked each box and transferred the contents into these cupboards. I have to admit I did consider itemising the contents of Cupboard A, Cupboard B, et cetera, but just the thought of it made me quite list-less!

This frenetic activity was monitored closely by the family cat who considers himself the most important member of the household. With a performance deserving of an Oscar, he can suffer a minor breakdown when he senses holiday season is on the horizon. At the first sign of suitcases, his large innocent eyes turn to small yellow slits, and the guilt trip he lays on us is difficult to ignore. 'They're leaving me again,' the look says, 'and I will have to put up with a stranger tending my needs. Although the she-human will leave peeled prawns and pink salmon, it is beneath my dignity to bow to bribery.'

I've always found Burmese wonderfully articulate, haven't you? But as we packed this time, there was no reaction.

'I think we've fooled him,' I said to Hon. 'He can't see suitcases so he hasn't put two and two together.'

Maybe this was the way to approach all our vacations in the future; just pack everything in cardboard boxes and the cat need not suffer separation anxiety.

5

After reading the brochures supplied with the van, it soon became obvious that setting off each morning would not be as simple as hopping in the cabin, buckling up the seat belt and switching on the engine. With great ceremony, Hon reached into his pocket and produced the Take-off Checklist. The rule was simple; the key was to go nowhere near the ignition until the check was complete. And as we positioned ourselves either ends of the van, I felt we were getting ready to take this baby into the skies.

'Cord disconnected?' the Captain asked.

I frowned. Why on earth would we connect the electricity while the van was stationery in the car park at home?

'I realise it's not connected at the moment,' Hon said, anticipating my question, 'but this is the first instruction when we're leaving the caravan park. We should familiarise ourselves with the sequence.'

Yeah, right!

'Steps raised?' he asked.

'Yes, sir.'

'Cupboards secure?'

'Sure are!'

At this stage they were as secure as they could be. But halfway through the holiday, when I started to get a trifle lax with the checking, we were in for a nasty surprise. As we turned a sharp corner, cupboard doors flew open and their contents sailed through the air. Luckily we were only attacked by a couple of the softer objects.

'Water pump off?'

I sighed. 'Well it will be – when we've switched it on.' My patience was wearing a little thin.

'Fridge switched to gas?'

'First thing I always do.'

'Cover down on the stove?'

'Does it look like it's up?'

'Aerial down and ventilation hatch closed?'

'Can't reach – you'll have to do it.'

At last the check was complete. We were feeling quite proud of our attention to detail. We had covered everything – well, almost.

After a rather sudden stop a few kilometres into the trip, the television fell off its lofty ledge and ended up suspended between the table and the sofa. It was then settled in its own chair, with a seat belt across its middle and an uninterrupted view of the highway. One more item was added to the checklist.

Hon turned on the ignition, carefully drove down the drive, and nudged the nose of the van onto the street.

'We can actually look down and see inside other cars!' I said, grinning. This was going to be wonderfully entertaining.

But we hadn't even reached the end of our street before I knew I would have more than enough to occupy me in our own vehicle. The roads suddenly appeared claustrophobically narrow, and I was starting to doubt whether they could accommodate our motorhome as well as other vehicles.

Hon prepared to overtake the car in front, so I dug my nails into the upholstery and leant heavily to the right, but this didn't make much difference.

'Watch out, you're too close!' I yelled. 'Oh God, they're too close! No, wait, don't try it yet – okay, well it worked that time.'

You may be wondering why LSD (Long-suffering Darling) didn't leave me on the side of the road ten minutes into the trip. All I can tell you is that the man is known for his incredible patience.

We soon cleared the busy suburbs and were travelling along the country roads, and these were so much wider than their suburban relatives that I could now remove my fingernails from the upholstery and relax.

When we initially sketched out a travel itinerary, I knew we were setting ourselves a fairly demanding task with the amount of kilometres we hoped to cover. I suggested we share the driving as it appeared too much for one person and casually mentioned this to the eldest son.

But his response was less than encouraging. 'You can't drive something that size, Mum. It's far too big for you to handle. Anyway, you'll never see over the wheel. And how do you expect to reach the pedals?'

Being close to six feet tall, he is convinced that life must be constantly challenging for his mother, who is yet to reach five feet!

'I'm sure the seats can be adjusted,' I said. No, this would be a breeze; I'd show him. But we'd only reached the end of our street when I knew he might have been on to something.

'I'm not really sure how I'm going to handle this when it's my turn,' I said, glancing at Driver Dan. 'Maybe I'll just wait until we're out on the open road, then I'll give it a go.' 'Open road' meant one straight stretch, with no other cars visible, and a tail wind.

'Don't worry, babe,' Hon said, 'I'm quite happy to do the driving. As soon as I sat in the cabin, I knew it would be too big for you to handle.'

While I was relieved to hear him acknowledge this, I was left feeling a tad inadequate. I wanted to be an equal partner in this road trip, but how could I contribute now? I suddenly caught sight of the large brown bag wedged firmly between the driver and passenger seats.

During the weeks of preparation, Hon had gathered every map and piece of information about the areas we would be travelling through and researched them thoroughly. (Yes, all right, maybe girls do end up marrying someone just like their dads!) But it was such extensive research, I knew he wouldn't retain every piece of information on each place we would pass through, and would therefore need my constant assistance. Yes, a very important job. And wedged amongst the maps and brochures was a selection of our favourite CDs and, next to that, a box of questions and answers from a favourite game we used to enjoy a few years ago.

'I shall be your ENO,' I proudly announced. Before he started making jokes about fruit salts and irregularity, I quickly explained. 'Your Entertainment and Navigation Officer.'

As we drove through Gawler and headed out along the Barrier Highway, I really felt our adventure had begun. Hon had adapted to his new driving role so well that all he seemed to lack was a microphone under his chin and a pair of aviator sunglasses. We passed through several small townships but it wasn't until we reached Burra, one hundred and fifty-six kilometres north of Adelaide, that we felt the need to stop and have a look around.

The economy of South Australia was approaching bankruptcy when copper was discovered at Burra, and a group of Adelaide traders nicknamed The Snobs made incredible fortunes extracting three hundred million dollars worth of copper from the mine. By 1851 Burra had more people living there than the combined populations of Brisbane and Perth.

Burra's Redruth Gaol was the first built outside Adelaide and housed about thirty prisoners. Extracts from the doctor's journal featured ailments such as 'silly, a little,' 'venereal eruption' and 'unable to walk to Adelaide'! One of the placards in the gaol gives an insight into the life of several female prisoners.

In 1919 three girls, Violet Benson, Ada Newchurch and Ursula Cruse were on the roof dancing, singing low songs, swearing downright insolence, destroying government property and exposing themselves to all passers-by in only their flannels and bloomers. You go, girlfriends!

The National Trust has been very diligent in Burra, and Market Square looks so much a part of the nineteenth century that it featured in the film *Breaker Morant*. The story was set during the Boer War (1899–1902) and starred many famous Australian actors.

Although there were still a few hours of daylight left after we had finished our tourist trail of the town, this would be the first night we had settled Winnie into a park for the night, and we were uncertain how long the Touchdown Checklist would take.

The local caravan park was in a perfect setting on the banks of the Burra Creek and, after parking at the entrance gates, we walked inside the small cabin which housed the reception area.

The man behind the counter glanced through the window and smiled. 'That's a monster you've got out there. Come far?'

'No, just Adelaide,' Hon replied. 'It's our first day on the road.'

With the 'eaves' experience still fresh in our minds, we requested a spot clear of overhanging tree branches, and the man insisted lot fourteen by the creek would fit our requirements. It did – sort of – but he failed to mention the forest of foliage we would have to manoeuvre around beforehand!

Suddenly my contribution to this trip became apparent. Ignoring Hon's protests, I hopped down from the van cabin and proceeded to walk slowly in front of Winnie. I was a 'scout', in the truest sense of the word, and was poised, ready to spot renegade eucalypts at a glance.

This activity soon attracted attention, and several grey nomads emerged from their caravans to monitor our progress. It didn't take long to realise we were in veteran vanners' territory. These mobile homes were set up to accommodate months of comfortable living, not just a few weeks escape from the rat race, and I was not about to be shown up.

As Hon finally pulled into our allocated spot, I was already thinking about our Touchdown Checklist and, seconds later, was pumped for action. 'Steps are down and the cord's connected,' I yelled.

Surely that wasn't a smirk on Driver Dan's face!

I disappeared inside the van and two seconds later stuck my head out of the door. 'Fridge switched to gas and water pump on.'

Obviously I was doing such a good job that Hon didn't feel the need to join in.

'Cover up on stove, and aerial raised.'

I was finding it difficult to wipe the smug expression from my face, so didn't even bother. And while this was going on, I was very aware of the elderly couple next door, who seemed fascinated by the whole production. They were sitting under their annexe, having a quiet drink before dinner and enjoying the unexpected entertainment.

'You've certainly got that down to a fine art,' said the nuggetty man in tired stubby shorts and a T-shirt telling all he was the World's Best Grandad.

'Yes, we don't allow ourselves to relax until we've been through our checklist,' I said, adopting a rather blasé air.

His wife, sporting the matching grandma shirt, walked over to the door of our Winnebago. 'It's so big – how many does it sleep?' she asked.

Thrilled to be able to show off, I invited the couple inside and gave them a detailed tour. They were particularly taken with the bathroom facilities, but nothing matched the look on their faces when I showed them the massive amount of storage space.

'You're very well organised, I must say. Obviously you know how important that is when travelling around,' Grandma said.

I smiled and nodded. She had decided I was a seasoned road warrior and I wasn't about to shatter the image. But then a familiar male voice seemed to resonate not only inside Winnie, but across the whole park, and all credibility was lost.

'Hey, babe, did you know we had a screen door?' Hon yelled.

The excitement of the first day took its toll, so after a meal at the local hotel, we were ready to settle down for the night. The main sleeping compartment of the Winnebago was lodged above the driving cabin, and comprised a double bed with small reading lamps and windows at either end. To maximise space, the bed had been designed across the van, with our heads over the right front wheel and our feet over the corresponding one on the left. This meant that the first one to climb into bed was trapped by the other body unless some careful manoeuvring was undertaken.

Once Hon closes his eyes, he is virtually comatose for the rest of the night. Unfortunately I suffer nocturnal restlessness (some call it a weak bladder), so it made sense for me to be closest to the stepladder. We had only been lying there two minutes when Hon groaned and threw a leg over me. I turned to him and smiled, but one look at his face made me realise he didn't want me – he wanted out.

'This isn't going to work,' he said, banging his head on the roof as he sat up. 'I can hardly breathe. Think I'll sleep on the sofa bed.'

And so, what initially appeared to be a 'divan à deux' soon turned into a solitary sleeping cell, and this arrangement continued for the rest of the holiday. And 'middle-aged' as that sounds, we had to admit we were a lot more comfortable.

The next morning I was woken by a squawking duck marching along the creek bank with her ducklings. Climbing from my eyrie, I took a cup of tea outside and watched the dawn break. Burra held a special place in my family's history. My father's maternal grandparents were well known in the district, and Dad spent every school holiday in this town. As I looked at the old trees hanging over the creek, I could almost imagine Dad as a young boy in scratchy woollen bathers, swinging from a rope across the river.

My daydream was interrupted by voices drifting across the still morning air. People were starting to emerge bleary-eyed from caravans, camper homes and tents, and the main topic of conversation appeared to be the weather. As I responded to their 'good mornings', I wondered what it was that made us much more casual with perfect strangers when we're on holidays. If we encountered the same people walking down the street back home, we would probably avert our eyes. Perhaps when you leave friends and extended family behind, you are anxious to share your experiences with others who will understand.

It was tempting to linger in this pretty town, but Driver Dan was keen to cover more countryside than we had on our first day. We wanted to spend the next night at Broken Hill and, as this was over three hundred kilometres away, we were back on the road by nine a.m.

As we travelled into the arid interior, the crispness of the morning soon thawed, and the shimmering mirage on the road warned of the hot day ahead. An hour into the drive, I was already bored with vast areas of 'nothing much', and when we started playing 'spot the roadkill', I knew it was time for the Entertainment Officer to step up to the plate.

As well as maps and brochures, the all-important brown bag contained a small blue box of cards. This was a selection of questions from a game we had at home, and when I packed it, I harboured visions of endless fun as we tested our general knowledge. But this pursuit proved anything but trivial!

Within seconds, we discovered you do not drive something the size of a pantechnicon round the countryside and expect to hear birds chirping outside. A force ten cyclone would have generated less noise, but being a 'glass half full' kind of gal, I plucked a card from the box.

'What river rises in Tibet, crosses Yunan, China, and makes its way through Laos, Kampuchea and Vietnam?' I yelled.

'Where does it rise?' Hon yelled back.

'Tibet.'

'And crosses where?'

'CHINA, LAOS, KAMPUCHEA AND VIETNAM,' I shrieked.

There was a slight pause.

'But what did you say about Yunan?' asked Driver Dan.

'IT – CROSSES – YUNAN,' I enunciated, in a dulcet roar.

The only other thing we could both hear distinctly was the sound of my teeth wearing down.

'WELL, YOU DIDN'T INCLUDE IT WHEN I ASKED WHERE IT CROSSED,' said Hon, who was now also talking in upper case.

And this was only question one!

I persisted for another five minutes, but you won't be too surprised to hear the box of questions ended up in the cupboard under the floor of the van. Thank God this was a fairly large area, as it became the receptacle for a lot of the stuff we swore we couldn't leave home without.

6

We had just driven through the small township of Olary, when I noticed Driver Dan frowning.

'What's wrong?'

'I was sure there'd be a petrol pump here, but apparently not. The next town is sixty-nine kilometres on. There's no way we'll make that,' he said, tapping the fuel gauge, which was heading towards the big E. 'I think we have enough petrol to get back to the town we've just been through. That's only thirty-eight kilometres – fairly sure I saw a petrol pump there.'

If he was trying to engender confidence, he had failed miserably, but our options were limited, so we turned around and headed back. During those thirty-eight kilometres, my eyes didn't leave the fuel gauge, as I watched for any slight movement, but finally we were pulling up at the lone pump in Manna Hill. The screen door of the adjoining hotel opened, and a neatly dressed woman in her forties emerged.

'Hi, folks. Can I help you?'

While she filled the tank, I walked across to the fairly plain structure which was the local watering hole. Opening the screen door, I stepped into the cool interior, and my jaw dropped.

The room was enormous, with a long antique bar to the right running the entire length of the room. To the left, an eclectic assortment of tables and chairs had been arranged to provide a lounge facility for the pub. One of the walls was completely covered in brown hessian. At first I thought it was dirty, but on closer inspection, realised the dirt was, in fact, many signatures and comments left by previous visitors.

The contents of the room covered nearly every decade of the twentieth century, and each flat surface was crammed with memorabilia. Kitchen scales, radios, cowbells, oil lamps, tin toys and porcelain dolls fought for their own space and even managed to overpower the full size church organ nestled in the corner. One particular collection had been deemed important enough to warrant its own glass cabinet. This was an assortment of fairies, angels, imps and elves, and I wondered if their glass prison was to stop them taking flight from their claustrophobic surroundings.

There were dozens of photos on every wall, but a large portrait by the doorway was the one to hold my attention. It was of a young woman in her late teens, dressed in a diaphanous gown which left nothing to the imagination. Quite risqué for the early 1900s, but her look of bravado was almost challenging the observer to object.

The door opened and the woman who greeted us earlier walked into the pub. 'Beautiful, isn't she?'

'Yes, very. Do you know the history of the photo?' I asked.

The woman smiled. 'That's my great-aunt, Eleanor Violet Field,' she said proudly. 'It's such a sad story, though.' With little encouragement, she went on to explain this lady's history.

'Eleanor was a professional actress and performed under the name of Vebby. She was the only girl in a family of five boys, and we think she may have adopted the stage name to save the family embarrassment at her choice of profession, rather dubious for those days.' She paused, and at first I thought she was trying to recall the rest of the story, but as she continued, it was obvious she relished this part of her family history.

'Vebby married Louis Hancock in 1916 but it didn't last very long. She then met Charles Martilch and the two lived together for many years, not bothering with the small details of ceremony and certificate.'

She paused once again and I could tell we were building up for the climax of this story.

'It was tragic in the end,' she said, staring at her great aunt. 'This was a true love match and, when Charles died, Vebby was heartbroken. She died in April 1946, and her body wasn't discovered for four days.'

I looked into Vebby's beautiful eyes and couldn't help feeling sad this woman's life had such an unhappy ending.

Vebby's great-niece realised she had a captive audience, and went on to share the history of the hotel. 'The first hotel was built in 1809 and over the years was burnt down twice,' she told me. 'But it was quickly rebuilt each time because it was a regular stopover for the Cobb and Co. coaches of the day.' She smiled. 'Enough about that – why don't you visit the toilets.'

I was startled at the sudden change of subject. Was she misinterpreting my intense concentration?

'The toilet?' I said.

'Through the passage at the end of the bar. You can't miss it,' she said, her smile taking on a mysterious quality.

And when I opened the door marked 'Ladies', I understood why. It was the standard smallest room of the establishment, but this had not curbed the owner's decorating enthusiasm in the slightest. The overall impression was a pastel palette of powder blue and pale pink. Ornate lace curtains covered the only window high up on the facing wall. A small table next to the toilet was covered in a matching lace tablecloth, and a profusion of stones, shells and crystals had been carefully arranged on top. Hand towels complimenting the colour scheme had been hung, placed or draped on every object.

Our diligent decorator had eventually run out of room but not ideas, so had turned her attention to the ceiling, where several baskets were suspended. These contained every example of artificial greenery to come out of an Asian sweatshop. Amongst these baskets were glass beads and glittering stars hanging from fine pieces of fishing line, and, to complement this look, a curtain of plastic beads had been hung across the doorway, with a smaller version gracing the toilet cistern.

It would certainly be a talking point for tourists popping in for a quick drink, but I could see a negative to this extravagant décor. I imagined long queues of desperate women standing in the hallway with legs crossed, while the present occupier of the smallest room took in the visual delights.

I stepped into the passage and Hon grabbed my arm.

'You have to see this,' he said, opening the door to the men's room, and nudging me forward.

I was standing on the doorstep of a jungle adventure. The walls of the room had been painted deep terracotta, with a butch version of the crystal curtain from the female toilet. This one was made of wooden beads and, even though I couldn't see it as a decorating option for our home, I had to admit it was quite effective against the rich earthy tones of the wall.

Two enormous prints of a leopard and a tiger fixed me with their feline gazes as they peered through a profusion of artificial plants. Several large brown pots had been placed at close intervals around the room and they held trees which would never shed their leaves. Each pot was perched on its own piece of plastic turf and, not content with just the plant, our decorator had nestled several ceramic animals at the base of each tree. I could understand the couple of monkeys and the coiled snake, but a psychedelic blue kangaroo? One could only assume some daring soul decided to try and extend the theme, but the three-foot-high black ceramic elephant standing in the corner soon drew our attention back to the Dark Continent.

This was impressive enough, but the *pièce de resistance* had to be the brass pole stretching from floor to ceiling, encircled by a brown stuffed chimp with moth-eaten fur and maniacal grin. And yes, there was a zip in the tummy for your pyjamas!

We walked back into the main area of the hotel and, as I picked up a business card from the counter, noticed the owners were Maxine and Dianne. I had a fifty per cent chance.

'Thanks – Dianne?' I said, and received a nod of acceptance. 'That's certainly been the highlight of our trip so far.'

But there was one more thing I needed to do before we left. I had noticed a box at the end of the bar with a note attached which read, 'Donate to the Royal Flying Doctor Service and leave your message on the wall.'

Placing some gold coins in the box, I grabbed the pen and headed for the hessian. I stared at the wall for a few seconds waiting for inspiration, but suddenly grinned.

'WE CAME – WE SAW – WE CONGOED' seemed to say it all.

7

Just because my first effort as Entertainment Officer had been a dismal failure, I was not going to be put off. This time I decided some music would be in order, so for the next one hundred and ninety-eight kilometres we meandered with Meatloaf, drove with Il Divo, ambled along to Andrew (Lloyd Webber, that is) and filled the van with Van (Morrison). Although I say it myself, the musical accompaniment could not be faulted and, as we approached the outskirts of Broken Hill, it was obvious the sigh emanating from Driver Dan was disappointment that my duets with each artist had come to an end.

Walking into the Reception area of the caravan park triggered a bell, and we could hear the muffled sounds of family dining emanating from the door behind the front desk.

A few moments later, a woman in her late sixties, with crisp, grey no-nonsense hair and an expression to match, walked through the door. Following close at her heels were two miniature poodles and three miniature children, all under five years of age – the children anyway.

'And what can I do for you good people?' she asked.

The excitement around her legs reached a crescendo, and I began to understand her weary expression. But just as we were about to reply, she threw us a look of apology.

'Sorry, I'll just get this lot sorted,' she said. Glancing at the carpet of kids and canines, she pointed towards the door. 'Kitchen – now – and that means everyone.'

The dogs, willing to accept a higher authority, took off, but the toddlers hesitated and exchanged looks. Their strength lay in numbers and resistance was being contemplated, but this granny had seen it all before.

'First one to finish their meal gets a Drumstick.'

The gust of wind created by their exit nearly blew us over!

'God love 'em,' she said, smiling, 'they're the joy of my life. Now, let's get you organised – one night, is it?'

'Yes, thanks. Have you got a vacant lot free of trees?' Hon asked, pointing at Winnie through the window.

'That's a big one,' she said, going on to assure us our allocated lot was tree-free.

We headed for the door and then I thought of something. 'Is there anywhere you'd recommend for a meal tonight?' I asked.

No, I hadn't forgotten about our own dinky little on-board kitchen, which had been the main attraction of the motorhome experience. Certainly it was serving its purpose with the breakfast bacon, and when the mid-morning munchies hit us. But was I really expected to cook a gourmet meal in an area the size of a cutlery drawer? (The fact that I rarely produced a gourmet meal in my more than substantial kitchen back home did not factor into the equation at all!)

'The Legions Club, love. It's a bit far to walk,' she said, and glanced through the window. 'And you won't want to move that monster once it's settled. When you're ready, give us a hoi, and I'll get the courtesy car to pick you up.' She smiled. 'By the by, the name's Diane.'

As promised, the lot was tree-free, and the second 'touchdown' was a smooth landing. So after locking the van we headed back to Reception. The courtesy car must have been hovering around the corner in anticipation as, no sooner than Diane had made the call, a lime green Torana pulled up in front.

A large woman unfolded her bulk from the driver's seat, adjusted her T-shirt around her ample stomach and hips, and showing off a large set of pearly beiges, fixed us with a smile. 'How ya goin'? Off to the club for a feed, are ya? Good choice. I'm Diane, by the way.'

At this rate, my memory could take a holiday as well! We settled ourselves in the back seat but before she started the car, she glanced over her shoulder.

'Don't mind some music, do ya?'

There were many small photos of Elvis covering the sun visor, a rubber effigy of the King bobbing around on a coiled spring attached to the dashboard, and a miniature pair of blue suede shoes hanging from the rear vision mirror, so I wasn't holding out for Beethoven's

Fifth! I commented on her obsession and she mistook me for a fan. Even suggested I get 'Love Me Tender' as a ring tone on my mobile phone.

So with the lovely Dianne accompanying her idol in an off-key duet, we all headed down to the end of lonely street to Heartbreak Hotel.

It's hard to believe both Hon and I had lived in South Australia for most of our lives but never visited Broken Hill. Known as The Silver City, this large rural town, sitting close to the New South Wales and South Australian border, still mines silver, lead and zinc, albeit from one mine only now. And no matter where you stand in the township, the large dumps and tall headframes associated with the mining industry dominate the skyline.

It started back in the late nineteenth century when a boundary rider named Charles Rasp was patrolling the Mt Gipps fences and discovered what he thought were deposits of tin. They turned out to be silver and lead, and this ore body became the largest and richest of its kind in the world. It was not documented whether Charles went on to make his fortune through this discovery, but mention was made of the name he was baptised with, which was Hieronymous Salvator Lopez von Pereira. One can only assume he wished to assimilate into his new environment, but what a pity to lose such an important-sounding moniker.

On our drive into Broken Hill the previous day, we had commented on the unique landscape with its contradiction of colours. The earthy terracotta of the plains had been brushed with the soft pastel blues, pinks and greys of the native foliage, and as we wandered through the many small art galleries in town we saw these colours duplicated on canvas.

Even if you have never been there, most people are aware of both aspects of this town, the mining and the masterpieces. But there was one thing I learned which fascinated me far more than any nugget or Pro Hart. Apparently Broken Hill was the scene of the only enemy attack on Australian soil in World War I. Initially I found it difficult to imagine how the enemy could have penetrated this far inland, and the story behind it brought tears to my eyes – tears of laughter.

In January 1915, four months before the Anzacs fought the Turks at Gallipoli, a trainload of Oddfellows from Broken Hill were on their way to a New Year's Day picnic in Silverton, when the train passed an ice cream truck flying the Turkish flag. Two men in the cart had rifles and it was assumed they were shooting rabbits, until they fired twenty to thirty rounds directly at the train. A railway truck marks the scene of the shooting and there is a replica ice cream cart at White Rocks, the scene of the shoot-out.

I just love the idea of the Turkish guys choosing an ice cream cart to launch their attack from. What a delight!

In its heyday, the small ghost town of Silverton, twenty-four kilometres west of Broken Hill, was a thriving mining centre of three thousand people. The current population is only about fifty, but many tourists visit each year. For quite some time it has been a popular location for filmmakers looking for a desert setting with easy access, and has been used in the films *Mad Max 2*, *Razorback*, *A Town like Alice* and *Priscilla, Queen of the Desert*, to name just a few.

The desolate feeling starts as soon as you leave Broken Hill, and the route to Silverton is a very ordinary stretch of road. But just as we were wondering whether the trip would be worthwhile, a lone building painted to blend with the ochre of the surrounding desert came into view, and minutes later we had pulled up in front of the Silverton Hotel, next to the low black car which Mel Gibson drove in *Mad Max*.

The interior of the hotel is one large room which serves as a museum to Silverton's film history. Each section of the wall depicts a particular film shot at this location. Even though the sun was nowhere near the yardarm, we ordered a couple of drinks and wandered outside to the beer garden. 'Garden' is a slight exaggeration, as the only visible green was some tattered shade cloth hovering above our heads.

I can vividly remember having to read the book *We of the Never Never* at school. This was an account of a young Victorian woman living in the city, who through marriage, moved to an outback station in the Northern Territory. As a liberated and radical teenager of the 1960s, I was horrified to realise she wrote under her husband's name (Mrs Aeneas Gunn), but was even more appalled to read the harsh conditions in the middle of our continent. When I think 'holiday' I think water, and some of my happiest memories involve swimming, snorkelling, fishing and lolling on a lilo. So when people wax lyrical about Uluru, I have to be honest and say that this big brown boulder could not leave me colder.

But as we sat sipping our drinks, the sun already showing its teeth, I felt oddly attracted to the beauty of this barren landscape. No wonder there were so many artists in the area. Nature's palette is truly amazing, and it was worth a second beer so we could drink it all in.

If we were going to make our next stop Cobar, however, we must reluctantly bid farewell to Silverton. We had only been driving for ten minutes when I realised I left my enthusiasm for desert landscapes back at Silverton. I switched on the radio, just in time to hear the lead item on the news broadcast.

> There was a robbery this morning at the local gardening centre where ride-on mowers and chain saws were some of the items taken. Police and fingerprint experts have attended the scene of the crime and an arrest is imminent.

The township where this crime occurred supported a population of merely seven hundred people, and I was in awe of the police expertise which could produce a couple of 'fingerprint experts' in such short time. Even this early in our journey, we had commented on the police stations in the country townships. Many were either the newest building in the main street or undergoing some sort of refurbishment, but suddenly it all made sense. With this sort of criminal at large, they probably felt it was money well spent.

The news and weather were followed by a comprehensive crop report, and if you still hadn't realised this was country radio, the advertising was a dead giveaway. There was no 'buy a dozen/get a dozen bottles free' deal at your local liquor store, and no providers offering mobile phone plans where you could talk to your friends for twenty-three hours straight and only pay a few cents. People out here were more interested in the cheapest stock feed prices, the most effective irrigation system and the dealership which had the best deal on tractors and utes. And you didn't need to be told all this in the melodious tones of the ABC. These voices were straight out of RADA, the Rural Academy of Dreary Announcers.

As well as advertising on radio, many companies had taken advantage of the endlessly boring scenery, and given the traveller billboards to read. One particular agricultural produce company had pulled out all stops.

> Gentlemen, Raise your Grasses!
> Don't Get Caught with your Plants Down
> Seed Cameras Used in this Area

My favourite rural sign, however, had nothing to do with advertising. It informed us that Stock on Road in Area Obey Signs. How on earth do they train them?

With all this to keep us amused, we were soon driving into Wilcannia, a township on the Darling River. In local Aboriginal dialect the name Wilcannia means 'a gap in the bank where the flood waters escape', and I was immediately in awe of a language that explains so much with so little.

Back in the 1880s, Wilcannia had a population of three thousand people. There were thirteen hotels and they even had their own brewery, The Red Lion. It was little wonder that the town was the centre of a number of coach routes, and two hundred and twenty-two steamers stopped there in 1887. Opals were found at White Cliffs in the 1890s and trade increased even more as Wilcannia became the central depot for the opal miners and the major recipient of their revenue.

Eventually road and rail traffic killed the steamer trade and the town's importance declined. But not before Wilcannia was hit with a rabbit plague at the end of the nineteenth century. The local children amused themselves on the way to school by exterminating many of these pests. But this became a problem in itself, so a man was employed exclusively to remove rabbit carcases from the streets. Someone who could genuinely make the statement 'All I ever seem to do is pick up after the kids'!

And Wilcannia wasn't without its visiting celebrities. The local courthouse was the scene of a case where Edward Bulwer Lytton Dickens (son of Charles) was one of the police magistrates, and Frederick James Anthony Trollope (son of Anthony, the famous novelist) was a prosecution witness. Now that's a case I'd love to have been a juror on.

The white population of Wilcannia is quite sensitive about travellers merely passing through their town and not staying. They maintain this is due to the number of indigenous people standing around in the main street doing precious little. I would like to assure the residents of Wilcannia (regardless of colour) that this had nothing to do with our decision to continue our trip and not stay overnight, but everything to do with the fact that Wilcannia is a godforsaken hole!

The monotonous scenery continued for the next two hundred kilometres, and combined with the heat haze shimmering on the road surface, the steady roar of the engine and the occasional 'splot' of an insect hitting the windscreen, the effect proved quite soporific. That was fine for me as I quickly nodded off, but by the time we arrived in Cobar, poor Driver Dan was exhausted. There had been a very strong wind, and with the open plain and the heaviness of the large vehicle, it took all his effort to keep Winnie on the road, and his arms had cramped with the effort. Holidays can be exhausting!

'Cobar is one of those deceptive country towns which can be driven through by those unaware of its charms or it can be a fascinating experience for those who pause...' I said, reading from the brochure the next morning.

Hon raised an eyebrow in lukewarm response.

'Do you want to know how Cobar was named?' I asked. Purely rhetorical, because I was planning to tell him anyway. 'Apparently a white man approached an old Aborigine and asked what he was doing. When he said he was making paint for a corroboree, the white man asked him where he'd got the paint from. The black fellow showed him the "gubar", which was a red ochre colour, and this turned out to be copper worth thousands of pounds. Isn't that fascinating – gubar/Cobar?'

'Riveting,' Hon said, as the other eyebrow joined the first.

But I was not fooled by his lack of enthusiasm. We both share an ability to remember completely useless facts, and I knew this would be brought up, even years later, at an appropriate time.

There wasn't anything else we wanted to check out in Cobar, so we were on our way once again.

8

The Riverside Caravan Park is nestled on the banks of the Bogan River at Nyngan and is all the brochure promises. But pretty as it was, I found a more important reason to stop there. Visitors were requested to 'drive slowly and keep an eye out for an eastern grey kangaroo called Sheena and in particular, a western red kangaroo called Reba, who is very small and quick'. And if you managed to avoid these meandering marsupials, there was another obstacle in the shape of Dino, the red kelpie, playing with his football!

It would have made a refreshing change from overhanging tree branches, but in the end our progress was unimpeded by either kangaroo or kelpie and, as soon as Hon switched the engine off, I had only one thing on my mind.

One of the main attractions of our motorhome was the idea of being completely self-contained. Not only did we have our own sleeping, cooking and relaxation areas, but complete bathroom facilities as well. The one thing about this, however, was the onerous responsibility we were taking on regarding our own waste matter.

The salesman had patiently explained the steps needed to keep our on-board toilet clean and hygienic and made the procedure look quite simple. He pointed to the locked compartment at the rear of the Winnebago and, showing us packets of chemicals, he appeared almost enthusiastic about emptying the small grey container.

'Winnie the Poo', as we named her, was in pristine condition when we took possession, and it was pointed out that if half-flushes were used most of the time, the receptacle would need emptying only every third day. I did wonder how they worked out that particular calculation. But the half-flush comment baffled us. On close examination of the cistern I could see only one button, and the same amount of water seemed to be dispensed each time this was pressed. But I wasn't that worried. I've never put much faith in half measures – for anything.

Our 'road commode' had a rather nifty feature where the user had the ability to swivel the seat at a forty-five-degree angle. With the bathroom being the size of your average broom closet, this enabled you to gain a few extra centimetres to dry yourself when stepping out of the shower, not to mention the wonderful change of scenery offered with each swivel. Arranging the seat face on and leaving the bathroom door open, you were able to look right down the length of the van to the driving cabin. This position became my personal favourite. The alternate view was facing toward the shower recess and, apart from the odd spider in the bathtub taking two steps forward and three back, it didn't offer much entertainment. And now here we were approaching the fourth night and Winnie the Poo had not been serviced.

I felt a certain urgency! 'Time to empty the loo,' I announced.

We walked to the back of the van, and with great ceremony and even greater awareness of the 'splash' factor, Hon carefully slid the grey box from its moorings. We walked down the path towards a sign which read 'Sewerage Station' and, gently placing the box on the lawn, my hero turned the yellow pipe around and released the cap.

'Are you ready?' he asked.

'Go for it,' I replied, a slight tremor in my voice, as I wondered what evils were about to be released. But I was pleasantly surprised. Liquid the colour and consistency of Evian water flowed from the pipe, and my relief was obvious. This, however, did not stop me from using half the contents of the River Murray to clean out the grey box a few moments later. You can't be too careful.

Bob (Bearer of Box) reached for the packet of chemicals. 'It says to use half a packet, but if we do that every three days we'll run out of chemicals before we get home.' He paused, and looked up. 'I think it only needs a quarter of a packet,' he boldly stated, challenging me to disagree.

My eyes formed narrow slits as I contemplated this statement, but the idea of running out of chemicals appealed even less. 'If you're absolutely sure,' I said, reluctantly.

With that serious task completed and the checklist done for the evening, we unfolded a couple of deckchairs and sat back with a glass of wine as we watched the sun set over the Bogan River.

'Surely they could have found a better name for such a pretty river,' I mused. 'I suppose back in 1835 it didn't conjure up mullet haircuts and flannelette shirts. Did you know the local Aborigines called it "nyingan", meaning "long pond of water"?' I was anxious to show off my local knowledge as I had read up on Nyngan before we arrived. 'Forget learning Japanese or German – we have the most sensible language right here in Australia.'

Having found our own little oasis, we were reluctant to go in search of a local club for dinner, so I made pasta in the van kitchen and we managed to finish two bottles of wine. Well, you can't take the chance they'll go off!

I woke to hear two distinct sounds, one discordant and the other melodious. The Richter-rated snoring emanating from the sofa bed was threatening to smash the crockery in the cupboards, but the laugh coming from the kookaburra sitting outside the van window was just as loud, and transported me back to East Adelaide Primary School. Every Thursday afternoon we had singing, and even though my voice was not one of the loudest, when it came to the chorus of 'Kookaburra sits in the old gum tree-ee', no one sang with more gusto.

But that was not the only nature calling! I decided to use the toilet in the park facilities so I wouldn't disturb the weary driver. (That wasn't the real reason but, you must admit, it makes me sound caring!) To be honest, I was still slightly bothered by the half dose of recommended chemicals Bob had used in Winnie the Poo.

The ablution block was beautifully clean and spacious, and there was even a vase of fresh geraniums on the vanity basin. Just before I walked outside, I looked inside one of the shower recesses.

Now I don't want you to think I had gone off our own 'on sweet felicities'. I still loved the idea of being completely self-sufficient, but the shower was a trifle restrictive. In order to wash your entire body, you needed to keep constantly mobile doing a little number I dubbed 'the recess rumba'. But with each movement, half the water from the shower rose would be deposited on the bathroom floor. The opportunity to be able to spread my wings was too good to miss. But I did wonder if I had the right outfit to be seen around the ablution blocks.

No matter where we went, there seemed to be a standard uniform worn by the female 'abluters' of the caravan parks. The minute the sun squeezed itself over the horizon, a veritable army of older women could be seen heading to the toilet block, dressed in floral brunch coats and towelling scuffs to match. I could only assume the Goodwill outlets around Australia had never-ending supplies of this particular fashion item, as you never see them in the department stores any more. And clutched to their chest was a shower bag the size of a small suitcase, adorned with tropical flora. I hoped my track pants, sweatshirt and leopard-print wash bag wouldn't stand out too much.

I felt I'd struck gold as I stood in the spacious shower cubicle with Niagara Falls beating on my head. But then I remembered the only other time I used a shower in a caravan park ablution block. It was a youth camp as a teenager and I still recall my mother's words of warning as she helped me pack.

'Always wear these in the public showers,' she said, tucking a pair of my brother's rubber thongs inside my bag, 'You don't want the skin between your toes to rot away, do you?'

Did she really expect an answer? This woman had a degree in maternal psychology, and knew that even though my brother's feet were considerably larger than mine, I would be prepared to endure any amount of teasing, rather than risk this dire fate.

Dragging my thoughts back to the present, I glanced down to check that none of my skin had disappeared down the drain, and heard the outer door open. Realising I was no longer alone, I became instantly water-conscious. As soon as I dried myself and dressed, I stepped out of the cubicle.

I smiled at the elderly woman applying an unnecessary layer of blush on already ruddy cheeks. Her hair had been over-coloured and over-curled over the years, and now there were only a few token wisps of grey to frame the deeply corrugated face. Large varicose veins striped their way down solid legs, which ended above surprisingly delicate feet. The small feet were spoilt, however, by gnarled toenails with chipped red polish on the end of toes which gripped the edges of well worn rubber thongs.

'Looks like another lovely day,' I said, smiling at her reflection in the mirror.

She looked pleased at the chance to chat. 'Yes, I was just saying to Ray, the tour'll be nice if that sun stays out.'

The blusher was now being applied to the neck region, and copious amounts of pink powder disappeared into the fleshy folds.

'Ray's m'neighbour – do a lot of travelling together, we do.'

I leant against the vanity bar. 'It's nice you have someone to travel with. Have you known each other long?'

'Yeah, been neighbours for years. Me old man died a few years ago.' She raised her eyebrows, and met my glance in the mirror. 'Good bloody riddance, I say. He was a bastard, that one.' She gave a humourless laugh. 'He'd be pissed orf knowing me and Ray were havin' a good time.'

The blusher had been replaced by lipstick, and it was proving a constant challenge to keep the fire engine red from disappearing into the deep crevices surrounding her mouth.

'Neder god on, dose doo,' she said.

I looked puzzled, so she gave up on the lipstick application.

'Me old man and Ray – didn't like each other. He reckoned I had a thing for Ray. Funny, that – I never did – still don't. S'just nice havin' someone to talk to. Ray's pretty quiet – don't say much.'

Perhaps Ray knew when the battle was lost! I asked if she had any children.

'Yeah, eight of the buggers. Old man'd never leave me alone. Must run in the family – got about twenty grandkids. Hang on – could be more like twenty-two. Never see 'em. Still, don't need the hassle. Better off without 'em.' The casual words didn't quite mask the flash of hurt in her eyes.

'Is your man good to you, love?' she suddenly asked.

'Yes, he's wonderful.'

She studied my reflection for a few seconds and nodded. 'Yeah, bet he'd never raise a hand to you, would he?'

Before I had a chance to reply, she continued, 'I can usually tell. You recognise the look. Had it meself for a long time. I can tell you for nothin', anything'd set him orf: dinner not on the table, kids too noisy, I'd cop it.'

No wonder the lines on her face were so deep.

'Anyway love, nice talkin' to ya,' she said, and left with a backward wave.

I walked back to the van in a contemplative mood. You could never tell what burdens people carried and, although I had only spent a short time in her company, I was glad this woman had found some happiness.

Hon was still sleeping but I was hungry, and the bacon and sausage aroma from neighbouring vans did their trick once again. As we ate, I decided to make two confessions to my road warrior.

The first was regarding the on-board shower, and how it had paled into insignificance once I discovered the Niagara Falls located in the ablution block. Hon's loyalty to everything regarding Winnie was usually unshakeable, but I did see a slight weakening in his resolve when I spoke in flowing terms of the water cascading upon my body and head.

The second confession concerned Winnie the Poo and I admitted there was reluctance to use said receptacle for even the quickest of visits. But Bob (Bearer of Box) stood firm, and assured me he had used enough chemicals.

Having cleansed my soul as well as my body, I located the brochure on Nyngan and began to read. 'You wouldn't believe it,' I said, laughing. 'There seems to be a theme running in this place. There's a story here about a bloke who got lost after straying from an expedition. He approached some Aborigines for food, and they initially made him welcome. But they became suspicious when he got up several times during the night, and they killed him!'

I looked up, and Hon was grinning. 'Sounds like a reasonable cure for nocturnal incontinence,' he said. 'You better watch out, babe.'

He had also found a brochure on the area, and was ready to match my story, and raise me one. 'Listen to this. Apparently Nyngan had the worst flood of the century in 1990. There was fifty million dollars worth of damage and a national relief fund was established.'

Is it any wonder that whenever I hear the word 'Nyngan', I also hear running water?

9

There appeared to be an unspoken agreement on the target we had set for this journey – 'let's get to the coast as soon as possible'. While the towns we passed through all had their own particular charm, we couldn't wait to hit the beaches of northern New South Wales. And so, when Hon suggested another long day of driving – and hey, don't underestimate the difficulty of being a passenger! – I was more than ready to meet the challenge.

'If you can do it, I can too,' I bravely stated.

When I reflect back on this particular day, I still wonder if I left my brain back in Nyngan. Or maybe God smote me because I used too much water in the shower! The first incident happened early in the trip when I was wearing my navigator's hat.

'Let's stop for coffee at Condobolin,' I said.

Hon frowned. 'Where?'

'Condobolin. I think we'll be ready for a break by then.'

His mouth was serious, but his eyes were a giveaway. 'Seeing we're not planning on going anywhere near Condobolin, you're probably right. Don't you mean Coonabarabran?'

I squinted at the map. 'Oh, yeah – why do they have to make the writing so bloody small?'

Selecting a CD, I sat back and watched the countryside flash by. The scenery had changed dramatically within several kilometres, and now we were surrounded by green instead of ochre.

As we passed through the small town of Gilgandra, I turned to Hon. 'How soon till we reach Condobolin?'

'Never, I hope – not on this journey anyway – but we'll hit Coonabarabran fairly soon.'

I groaned. 'Shades of my mother,' I said, with little humour. Mum had suffered Alzheimer's in the latter stages of her life, and I had yet to speak to a doctor who could assure me it was not hereditary.

'I think this town needs a new name,' Hon said, seeing me frown. 'How does Condoblabran sound?'

When we stopped for our caffeine fix (I had double-strength), I couldn't resist glancing at the brochure to glean my one odd fact related to this town.

'This'll do,' I said, striking gold. 'What's the name of Australia's only Chinese bushranger, who was active in this district in the mid-1800s?'

Hon stared out the window, and then suddenly smiled. 'Ned Kerry.'

'Very droll! Nup, it was Sam Poo.'

These brochures served their purpose and were a constant source of information about the places we visited. But unlike the retired couples with no time constraints, we only had a few weeks, so our sightseeing had to be pared accordingly. And that's how we discovered Information Centres!

As we drove into a larger town, my navigational radar was switched to full alert, and I would scan the horizon looking for the blue sign with the white 'I'. Often these centres were located in a small building set in a park in the centre of town. They were run by an assortment of retirees who had lived around the area for many years, and these people took great pride in sharing their local knowledge.

'And where are you folks from?' was the standard welcome. The further east we travelled the more enthusiastic was the response to our answer of Adelaide.

'Weeell – you have come a looooong way.'

I wondered if they kept an extra store of enthusiasm for any visiting Russians!

As soon as we asked about the tourist attractions, they would grab a local map, and with the help of a black felt pen, draw a large cross.

'You are here!' they would announce, and then pause dramatically while we took in that piece of startling information.

This procedure was repeated so often I became convinced this must have been Rule 1 in the Volunteer's Handbook, and they soon became the 'You Are Here' centres.

Having established where we were, these rapturous retirees would start their sales pitch on where we could be. Each town seemed to possess at least one outstanding feature the volunteers were proud of, and we usually found it worthwhile to follow their advice. And so it was with a fair amount of confidence we approached the You Are Here centre in Tamworth.

As we walked up to the counter, a retired gentleman smiled and reached for a map.

Taking a large black felt pen from his top pocket, he made the obligatory cross with a rather dramatic flourish. 'You are here,' he stated, and we relaxed into the comfortable familiarity. He then glanced up, his eyes darting between the two of us, and after a rather long and embarrassing pause, seemed to reach a decision. 'There's quite a bit to see in our wonderful city, but I'm getting the feeling you folks are on limited time. Would I be right?'

We gave synchronised nods.

'So let me just point out a few highlights.' The first black line shot out at right angles to the cross. 'This is the Anglican church, a nice bit of architecture and over a hundred years old. Well worth a look.'

His pen returned to the cross and another line was added. 'The Catholic church is not as old, but the windows are a treat, done by a local chap some years ago. Don't think he was even of the faith, but did a great job.'

A third line was added. 'Now – the Uniting!' He paused to check whether anyone was in earshot, and his voice lowered a tone. 'They can call it what they like, but it will always be the Presbyterian to me. I don't know why they had to send the Methodist and Congregational people over to us. We had enough worshippers in the first place. What's wrong with keeping them separate, eh? Tell me that!'

Both Hon and I stared at the map with almost manic concentration. I was wondering how long this ecclesiastical exercise would continue before I let forth with some heavy cursing I would have to pass off as Tourette's, but fortunately our friend capped his pen.

'So there you are,' he announced, 'that'll be all you'll have time for if you really take in the beauty of each one, don't you think?'

Well, yes – if you're on safari for your lost soul! But why didn't he mention the twelve-metre-high golden guitar we passed on the way in? The one standing outside a museum where Tex, Smoky and Chad had been immortalised for posterity? Maybe he felt country music to be the work of the devil!

I can't speak highly enough of the You Are Here centres, and even in his misguided way, our gentleman in Tamworth was supplying the information he thought we needed. But I couldn't say the same for the volunteer we encountered further on in our journey.

The last thing I would want to do is cast 'nasturtiums' on this wonderful country town, so the exact location will remain a secret. I'm sure it was a one-off incident and things would have been restored to normal the next day. But when we walked into this particular centre that day, I did a double take. Instead of the usual face wrinkled into a welcoming smile surrounded by a cap of grey, a girl in her late teens sporting electric-blue hair, black nail polish and large nasal ring was lounging behind the counter. She glanced up and lazily rearranged the wad of chewing gum into the opposite cheek. 'Can I help youse?' she said in flat, nasal tones.

I placed my jaw in a more attractive position, and smiled. 'I hope so. We were wondering about the tourist attractions in this area.'

''Snot a lot really.' Her nasal ring had developed a life of its own.

Hon had already highlighted an attraction in one of the brochures. 'We thought we'd like to take a look at this,' he said, 'How do we get there?'

'Oh, that,' she said, her eyes clouding over as she contemplated how anyone could find this of the slightest possible interest. She raised her arm and pointed to the window, and a deafening clank of metal bangles echoed across the room. 'Ya sorta go up that road for a way, and then you turn left, and then I think it's right at about the – er, one, two, three – yeah, the third street – no, hang on, might be the second street and then…'

I held up my hand to stem this intellectual discourse. 'What about a local map? You know, the ones you put a cross on and say "You are here"?'

Did I really have to teach this girl her job? After fiddling under the counter for several minutes, she finally produced something we recognised.

'This it?' she asked, pushing the map across the counter.

At last we were getting somewhere! I was tempted to say 'Good girl' and promise her an elephant stamp, but then she wrecked it all.

Picking up a fine-tipped biro, she made the smallest cross I'd ever seen. 'That's us,' she announced.

I silently wished bifocals on her before the age of thirty.

With gargantuan effort, Kelly Osbourne managed to raise her heavily mascaraed eyelashes a fraction and glance in our direction. 'Think it's closed on Froideese,' she said.

'And that would then allow them to open all day Satdee and Sundee, roight?' I desperately wanted to ask.

'It says here "Open Wednesday to Sunday from nine a.m. to five p.m.",' Hon said, pointing to the fine print. 'Would this be a current brochure?'

Her lashes crashed to her cheeks. 'Oh – yeah!'

I'd had enough. 'Thank you for your help,' I said, manufacturing an expression which could be taken for a smile – or not. 'It's been very – informative.'

Hon's eyebrows almost hit the ceiling, but I hadn't finished.

Just as we were about to step outside, I turned and smiled at her. 'And I do hope your grandmother gets well soon. Tell her she's sorely missed.'

Back at Tamworth, we had a decision to make. Although we were hardly fans of country (or western) music, we were not too excited about the 'God Trail', so the only thing left was to 'dance with the devil'. We acknowledged that a visit to Tamworth would have been incomplete if we had not checked out the Golden Guitar Museum. Even before we pulled into the car park, I knew I would be asking Driver Dan to snap a shot of me next to the highly strung monument which graced the front of the museum.

I love big things. It wasn't until I was updating the photo albums that this dawned on me, and I couldn't deny that I had pointed to, embraced and stood next to the following.

>The biggest rocking horse in the world (Gumeracha, South Australia)

>An enormous cod (Swan Hill, Victoria)

> A huge piece of citrus fruit (Berri, South Australia)
>
> A frighteningly big crustacean (Kingston, South Australia)
>
> The Tallest Man In the World (Ripley's Museum, Gold Coast)

To be honest, the last one wasn't a good photo of me. I had just turned sideways and realised my eyes were level with his crotch!

And it's not as if I even look at these photos once they are in the album. But at the time there is something almost irresistible about the 'kitschness' of it all.

And the Golden Guitar did not let me down. It was modelled on the trophy which has been presented at the Australasian Country Music Awards since 1973. There are many definitions of country music in the information brochures the museum provides. Some people feel it is defined by its simple chord progression and memorable chorus. Others highlight the strong storyline accompanied by a simple and memorable chorus, as in the famous songs *Pub With No Beer* and *The Band played Waltzing Matilda*. I preferred some of the simpler definitions:

> 'if it sounds like country, it is'
>
> 'it must sound like Tex, Buddy or Slim in the 40s and 50s'
>
> 'if the cheque comes from Nashville, it's country'

We wandered through the Wax Museum and were impressed with the time and effort put into the figures. In the early days, the original figures were made in Nashville, USA, but it's good to know the latest ones are now made in Australia.

The Roll of Honour lists show the annual winners of the Golden Guitar Music Awards and, even to a couple of 'city and eastern' aficionados, the names Slim Dusty, Smoky Dawson, Becky Cole and Keith Urban were very familiar.

Yes, Tamworth was certainly worth the stop and we were pleased we decided to dance along the road to ruin instead of the road to Damascus.

10

'How long do you think it will take to get to Armitage?' I asked.

I didn't even have to see the smirk on Hon's face to know I'd said the wrong thing. Apparently I was still suffering brain drain from that infernal water at Nyngan.

'You know where I mean – Armidale,' I snapped.

This man I live with has the most shocking memory I've ever come across. Most of the time it just doesn't exist, and reminders about pocketing his mobile each morning before he leaves home are forgotten thirty seconds later as he disappears through the door. But I knew that somehow, this day of verbal stuff-ups would stay firmly lodged in his memory.

Armidale is a very pretty spot and apparently looks so good in autumn they feel it is worth a special celebration. The city is known for the University of New England, appropriately named, as it did remind me of that area in the USA. 'Heritage' is a word frequently used when talking about the different attractions of this city. You can take a free Heritage Trolley tour or a Heritage Walk, the buildings are of Heritage Value and every brochure stresses this area is rich in – you guessed it – Heritage.

Armidale is only a two-hour drive from the coastal city of Coffs Harbour, and acts as a draw card for students trying to decide where to study for their academic careers.

We headed for the centrally located Pembroke Tourist and Leisure Park. From the first glimpse of the landscaped gardens, green lawns and beautiful trees set on fourteen acres, we were not surprised it had won an Inland Park award. I had exhausted my culinary skills with the one or two meals I had prepared up to this stage, so when Hon suggested dinner at the bowling club, I wasn't about to argue.

No sooner had we stepped inside the door of the club than a gentleman in bowling whites walked up and welcomed us. We learnt this was not an official duty but one he had taken upon himself. With almost manic enthusiasm, he pointed out the bar area, 'You'll be ready for a cold one, I bet', the gentleman selling raffle tickets, 'You can't win it if you're not in it, right?' and the queue for ordering meals, 'Wait until you taste the tucker – can't recommend anything really,' a slight pause accompanied by a wink, "cause it's all good.'

We smiled our thanks and hoped 'Jack High' wasn't waiting for a dinner invitation, but he had already spotted more visitors. We grabbed one of the few remaining vacant tables, ordered a pre-dinner drink, and Hon joined the queue to place our food orders. Suddenly I was conscious of a young lad standing to my left.

'Wanna buy some raffle tickets? You can win heaps of cool stuff,' he said, pointing to a slightly raised area at the edge of the room. Judging from the numerous meat trays precariously balanced on frail looking card tables, the 'cool stuff' comprised chops, sausages and steak. And from the size of each tray, one could only assume the local butcher was a generous soul, or maybe just a lawn bowls fanatic. But did we really want to cart an entire cow around in Winnie for the next few weeks? I glanced back at the lad with an apologetic smile, but suddenly I was looking at my youngest son, with his course dark blond hair and direct blue-eyed gaze.

'I'll take a book, thanks.'

When Hon joined me at the table once more, he noticed the tickets, looked towards the stage area, and raised his eyebrows.

'Don't worry,' I quickly said, 'there's going to be fifty draws and they can't all be meat trays.'

'You know this for a fact, do you?' he said.

I suddenly had an awful vision. I was frantically tearing the plastic wrap from a tray and doling out six chops, four sausages and a piece of rump to each person in the bowling club! But half an hour later when number forty-nine was called, I grabbed one of our tickets and sprinted to the front of the room. As I joined Hon at the table two minutes later, I didn't even bother trying to hide the smug grin.

'Sorry, darling, I know you wanted a meat tray – maybe next time!' I said, slapping a $20 petrol voucher in front of him.

With this sort of success, there was no stopping me. The first thing I did on arrival at subsequent clubs was to locate the raffle ticket seller. Hon still felt that some day we would be cooking a barbecue to feed the entire township, but the only other prize we snagged was nothing to do with meat. We won a dinner voucher for a meal at the bowling club where we had just dined. When they found out we had already eaten and would be leaving tomorrow, they swapped it for a $20 petrol voucher. At this rate, we'd soon be driving the highways of Australia on free fuel! No wonder lawn bowls is experiencing a surge of popularity.

I loved the feeling of Armidale and, as we strolled back to the park, I was tempted to suggest we extend our stay in this gentle, laid-back place. But we were only two hours from the coast and I could almost smell the salt spray. If we were going to extend our stay anywhere, it would make more sense to be within sight of the ocean. And so we headed to Ballina – well, sort of. Firstly, I owed Hon a favour.

11

Much as I hated admitting it, life on the road was starting to appeal. Maybe it was genetic. My mother always claimed my grandmother 'had a bit of the gypsy in her'. I suspect this statement had more to do with her penchant for colourful jewellery, and a lot of it, rather than her wanderlust, however.

Although we were limited by the number of weeks we could stay away, the pace we set each day was our own. Just because our rough itinerary designated we would spend the next night at a certain town did not necessarily mean this had to be strictly adhered to. We were constantly attracted by the many brown and white signs along the highways denoting a particular tourist attraction which must be checked out. Often these would lead to well known tourist features of the area which we had pinpointed for a visit anyway, but many of these signs highlighted a spectacular view, a nature trail or a geographical feature.

Hon was adamant. He was not going to bypass any of these signs, just in case it was the one we should not have missed. So each time a brown sign loomed in the distance, you could almost smell the excitement in the van (only from the driver's side, I might add!) And, based on other holiday experiences, the attractions Hon found absolutely irresistible were the blowholes.

We would stand at a railing (me clinging) and stare at the water as it was sucked into the hollow of the rocks, and after a pause filled with excited anticipation, watch the water suddenly erupt into the air in a spectacular fountain.

I say 'spectacular', but not all of them could be categorised this way. Some only produced a mere 'phfft' rather than the obligatory 'whoosh', and at these times, Hon experienced deep disappointment. I had no idea there were so many of this geographical phenomena around Australia but, even if I had, I know I would not have displayed an uncontrollable urge to compare each one.

And so the day Winnie veered off the highway at the umpteenth brown blowhole sign, I saw red. 'Right, that's it,' I said, through clenched teeth, 'I've had enough blowholes to last a lifetime. Stop the van, I'm getting out.'

I must admit I hadn't really thought this through. We were out in the middle of nowhere and the next town was at least an hour's drive away. What did I think I was going to do? You're right – thinking didn't play a large part in this. I could tell by the look on Driver Dan's face that he was contemplating whether to put his foot down, literally and figuratively, but after a few tense moments, he turned Winnie around and headed back to the highway.

I know what you're thinking. It wouldn't have hurt me to see another blowhole – and you're probably right. I did have a guilty conscience and coyly admit my outburst was rather childish. But my man did get his own back. He never missed an opportunity to remind me that his life was less than complete due to a gap in his blowhole knowledge. So when he asked if I wanted to see the Standing Stones of Glen Innes, I was desperate to show I had matured beyond belief. And that's how karma works!

Up to this point, I thought the blowholes of this world were fairly boring – but at least they do something! Standing Stones – the name really says it all. They are a pile of stones, and yes, they are certainly standing – rather like a poor man's Stonehenge – but because I was making up for my 'blowhole bust-up', I wanted to do this thing properly.

On the grounds of the Standing Stones, there is a tiny crofter's cottage housing the local information centre (you are here and this is where you want to be) so, after picking up a brochure, we wandered amongst the monoliths.

The stones are in recognition of the contribution made to Australia over the last two hundred years by people with Celtic origin, and is the only cultural gathering place in the world for the Celts. There are thirty-eight of these granite monoliths, each weighing roughly seventeen tonnes.

At first you get the impression the stones have been laid at random, until you read the literature. Each one has its significance, ranging from the twenty-four in a circle representing the hours of the day to the four cardinal stones marking the compass points and seven stones in solar alignment. These stones surround three central ones, the northern representing the Gaelic-speaking Celts from Ireland, Scotland and the Isle of Man, the southern representing the Celts of Wales, Cornwall and Brittany and the gold-coloured stone representing the Australians.

Although I could feel the warm sun penetrating my T-shirt, it wasn't difficult to visualise the ceremony held in May celebrating the Australian Celtic Festival, when a lone piper stands in the early morning mist and heralds in the dawn. My imagination was running riot and I was so into this particular tourist attraction, I could almost see the pagan rituals they would perform in the depth of night, complete with wailing virgins and even louder wailing goats. They very wisely omitted this information from the tourist brochure, however.

We walked back to the car park and I was amazed to find we had spent nearly an hour looking at big rocks. Yes, I had to admit it, I was captivated – and my conscience was appeased. But it didn't mean I changed my view on blowholes!

When we mapped out our route all those months before, I was pleased to see we would be near the town of Tenterfield, Peter Allen's birthplace. I can first remember seeing him on Brian Henderson's television show *Bandstand* back in the sixties, when he and Chris Bell performed as the Allen Brothers. But it wasn't until Peter Allen embarked on a solo career in the early 1970s and wrote some wonderful music, that I really took notice of him.

At first there was reluctance by the people of Tenterfield to accept him as one of their own. Openly gay, he married then divorced and divided his time between New York and Los Angeles, and this lifestyle was hard to understand in a small rural township in Australia. But when his popularity grew and the tourist flood into Tenterfield began, the citizens embraced their international son. His fans believe when he sang 'forgiveness is a funny thing, it warms the heart and cools the sting', that he was referring to his acceptance by the city fathers of his home town.

There can be no doubting the effect this town had on the small sad boy known as Peter Allen Woolnough. His relationship with his grandfather George is so poignantly revealed in the words of one of his best-known songs, 'The Tenterfield Saddler'.

It didn't take long to locate the saddlery on High Street, where George Woolnough worked from 1908 until his retirement in 1960. One of his most famous customers was A.B. Banjo Paterson, the well-known Australian poet and author, who lived in Tenterfield for a short while after marrying a local girl.

The Tenterfield Saddlery was classified by the National Trust of Australia in 1972. The doors and woodwork are of red cedar and, apart from the maintenance, is in its original condition. It is still a working saddlery and easily transports you back through the years when this was an essential part of many outback towns. But I was anxious for the more recent history of Tenterfield.

The Peter Allen Museum is located in the You Are Here centre and looked after by a woman named Patty. When she realised I was a fan of this Aussie legend, she allowed me to have my photo taken holding Peter Allen's maracas, the same ones he used when he recorded 'I Go to Rio'. Apparently one fan was so overcome when she first spotted them, she dissolved into tears. (No, it wasn't me.)

12

Hon had 'stood with stones' and I had 'mariachied with maracas' – it was time to head for Ballina, our next overnight stop. I had breathed enough brown dust to last a lifetime and was ready to inhale the salty spray of the south Pacific. But apparently we had to earn our piece of paradise!

The road between Tenterfield and Casino is 'a long and winding', and would be hairy enough if travelled in a normal sedan. But in Winnie, it became positively terrifying. Lismore is about halfway between Tenterfield and Ballina and most travellers use this as a convenient break. Lismore locals say they can pick the tourists coming in from Tenterfield by the sway in their walk. After a calming cup of caffeine, we joined the Bruxner Highway and were relieved to find it was a straight stretch of road, and our arrival on the eastern side of the continent was as smooth as silk.

There are probably about a dozen caravan parks in Ballina, a testament to the number of people holidaying in this beautiful spot. But as soon as we saw the Ballina Lakeside Park, our minds were made up. Situated on the lake front, there was a break wall to the river on one side and a seven-hundred-metre walk to the beach on the other. As we pulled into our lot, the smell of barbecue meat was almost overpowering and our saliva glands began working overtime. But first things first – there was another more urgent matter niggling at the back of my mind.

Although we were always fairly confident everything in Winnie was secure and fastened down after our morning checklist, the crazy winding ride between Tenterfield and Casino had still managed to dislodge several items, and the ride had been accompanied by the sporadic clunk of doors opening and items hitting the floor. But this wasn't my main concern. I was listening for the splash of liquid, and wondering how Winnie the Poo was coping with the unnecessary agitation.

We were due to perform the second emptying 'ceremony' at our next overnight stop, but the suspense was killing me. I walked over to Bob (Bearer of Box), who was already armed with a pack of loin chops and barbecue tongs, ready for another sort of action.

'Sorry, Hon, but I won't be able to relax if we don't empty Winnie the Poo tonight.'

'But we only emptied it a couple of nights ago,' he said, adding some sausages and rissoles to the pile of meat.

'Yes, I know, but I want to make sure your chemical equation is working.'

Don't you love it, girls, when you see 'that look' come over your husband's face? You know the one – 'I may as well do it now, 'cause there won't be a moment's peace until I do!'

And so for the second time, we opened the small door at the back of the van, slid out the box, and Bob carried it to the sewage station. He removed the cap, pointed the pipe and the contents started to empty into the drain.

And that's when I screamed! 'Oh my God, that's revolting!'

Several families nearby glanced up from their meal, and frowned.

'What happened to the Evian water?' I screeched. 'Look at it. It's the colour of – oh no, I'm going to be sick – it's the colour of – poo!'

Chops and sausages hit plastic picnic plates, but I was beyond caring about people's sensibilities.

'I knew you should have put more chemicals in,' I said, my voice a dulcet roar. 'What on earth were you thinking, making up your own instructions?' The look I gave Bob could have cut through steel. 'Right, that's it. I'm in control of the chemicals. Where are those packets?'

The flush-out I had given the grey box two days earlier was nothing compared to the cleaning it now underwent. Satisfied we could serve our dinner from the inside of the box should we wish, I then opened the packet of chemicals and threw the entire contents inside. 'There, we'll have none of that happening again.'

LSD (Long-suffering Darling) shook his head, and muttered something about running out of chemicals before we arrived home, but I wasn't concerned with the future; the immediate problem had been solved.

And let me just say that the next sewage stop proved that my 'extravagant' use of chemicals was a wise move. The Evian water made a stunning comeback!

Yes, well, all right, I'll come clean. We did run out of chemicals well before we arrived home. But after my first encounter with the wonderful character in the toilet block, the roomy shower recesses, plus a sewage problem I could leave behind for someone else to worry about, I had come up with my own ablution solution.

We eventually had our barbecue and thoroughly enjoyed it. I can't say the same for the other residents of the park. Soon after my outburst, there was the unmistakable sound of plates being scraped and plastic bags hitting the bins.

I woke early the next morning and couldn't wait to explore this beach-side gem. I missed my morning beach walks since leaving home and, although the air was still fresh at this hour, they had promised a temperature in the high twenties later on. Quite a few people had the same idea, and I recognised the elderly couple walking towards me along the beach, as fellow park residents.

'Good morning,' I smiled. 'Too nice to stay in bed, isn't it?'

'Yes,' the man said, 'it's such a lovely spot we're finding it hard to tear ourselves away. Still, we're a couple of free souls,' he said, smiling down at his wife, 'so we don't have a schedule to follow.'

'How I envy you,' I said. 'Oh well, better keep up the momentum,' I added, anxious to keep walking. 'Have a good stay.'

Before I had taken more than three steps, however, the woman's voice echoed behind me.

'Excuse me, dear. Did you get your little problem sorted out last night?'

I felt the colour start around the base of my neck and slowly seep into my face until perspiration pricked my scalp. Just before we settled down the night before, I showed Hon a rash that had developed in a rather intimate area. We had made several lewd suggestions regarding my ailment and the treatment we felt it needed, and this personal conversation was now replaying in my head. Surely my voice hadn't carried through the walls of Winnie and across the entire caravan park. But then the penny dropped! This couple had obviously witnessed the Winnie the Poo ceremony, and that was nearly as embarrassing!

'Yes – thanks – everything is sorted,' I said, looking a trifle apologetic. 'I hope we didn't put you off your meal.'

The woman smiled. 'Not at all, dear. We were still laughing about it hours later.'

When I arrived back from my walk, Hon had started preparing breakfast. We had the usual discussion about the day's activities, but I could tell Driver Dan was reluctant to head off sightseeing immediately. I suddenly realised what a wonderful driving job he'd been doing, some days covering a huge number of kilometres. It would do him good to unwind and settle somewhere for more than one night.

13

Friends who had visited Ballina recently were adamant we should experience breakfast at the Shelley Beach Café, a short distance from the township. They didn't elaborate, so we were surprised to find a small, rather ordinary kiosk, perched on a cliff top overlooking the beach.

It was early morning, but as we tackled a large plate of bacon and eggs, the sun already promised a warm day as it glinted on the sleek grey shapes of the dolphins breaking the surface of the water. We even spotted a lone whale further out to sea, and both agreed this was the perfect way to start our day. We were tempted to linger over a second coffee, but the You Are Here lady had been insistent. 'You must see this – and this one too – and oh yes, make sure you don't miss this one,' she had said, thrusting a myriad of brochures at us. Her enthusiasm had been infectious, so with a last glance at the early morning mariners, we headed off.

First stop was Thursday Plantation, a business devoted entirely to the wonders of tea tree oil. The only thing I knew about this natural plant extract was its antiseptic qualities, and I went through many bottles when the children were small and accident-prone. But as we walked into the small brick building which housed the shop, I was confronted with more information about the produce of the melaleuca tree than I knew what to do with.

The local industry was started in 1927, and the oil had enjoyed periods of popularity throughout the years. During World War II, the Australian government commandeered all stocks for the military, and this was used in everything from the soldiers' first-aid kits to being mixed with machine cutting oil in the munitions factories. Apparently this dramatically reduced instances of dermatitis. I wondered how many men contemplated the profession of tea tree cutting, as this immediately made them exempt from military service!

There was a slump in demand for tea tree oil until the 1970s, when people became more aware of pollution and the hazards of synthetic chemicals. Interest in natural alternatives became popular and the trend has only increased over the years.

This miracle oil promised to do everything from cleaning floors, removing chewing gum from hair, healing sore throats, easing muscular pains and even relieving jock itch. I bought the largest bottle I could find. But when we eventually arrived home, I had lost all interest in cleaning floors, my children had grown out of chewing gum, this was the first winter we had not suffered sore throats and when my 'musculars' ached, I was so busy complaining, I forgot to treat them. But I'm still looking round for a sporting stud who needs relieving!

We wandered outside and followed the signs to the Rainforest Walk and Sculpture Garden. The East Coast Sculpture Show is a yearly exhibition of about eighty contemporary works. While they were all clever, one in particular attracted my attention. It was titled *The Kneeling Woman*. The figure was naked, displaying full drooping breasts, a large, rounded stomach and solid thighs. As if this wasn't spooky enough, each of her hands was cupped around a more than generous butt cheek. I could have been looking in a mirror, and felt thrilled someone else had acknowledged the beauty of overeating and not enough exercise.

But the Rainforest Walk beckoned, and we paused to read the warning sign about the snakes, lizards and spiders we could encounter.

Hon was astounded when I started down the path, without any hesitation. 'Are you sure you want to do this?' he asked.

'Yes, of course,' I said. 'Surely you're not nervous?'

'No, course not – but I know how much you hate snakes.'

'Probably won't even see any,' I said. 'Come on, let's go.'

I know you think I'm brave – facing my demons head on – but I did have a helper in the form of a secret weapon. You see, I really believed the tea tree oil possessed magical qualities, so had removed the lid and was ready to cope with any situation we would encounter. And it worked! We didn't come across any snakes or lizards, although there were several large webs strung across the path. Even though these webs hung quite low, this didn't worry me. Men like to feel they're in charge, so naturally I let Hon lead the way!

Next stop on the tourist trail was Macadamia Castle, and from a distance I was very impressed with the grandeur of the place. It displayed the obligatory battlements and moat, but as we approached the drawbridge, it looked a trifle tawdry. Not that it mattered, as the real interest lay inside.

The literature promised this was a temple to the humble macadamia and it didn't lie – this was the largest nut display I had ever seen. Actually it was the only one I'd ever seen. South Australia boasts an almond festival but, as is always the case in your own home state, you rarely play tourist.

Like tea tree oil, I had managed to exist without macadamia nuts in my life, but apparently I was in the minority. Australia's domestic and export macadamia crop is worth over $100 million annually. It's the world's most nutritious nut, and not only does it contain no cholesterol, it even encourages weight loss. And the brochure also informed me that 'Australia has a reputation for premium quality nuts.' I'm pretty sure I've met a few!

It could have been the aroma of roasting nuts, but half an hour later we left the castle reeling under a 'mighty mass of macadamias'. We had every situation covered, from the lightly salted for pre-dinner drinks, the unsalted for cooking, the chocolate-coated to have with after-dinner coffee and the magnetised for the fridge. I even found some crafted into earrings, but you have to stop somewhere.

The final attraction for the day was situated in the hinterland just outside Byron Bay. The Crystal Castle sounded irresistible:

> ...you will discover Australia's most spectacular treasure trove of natural crystals and beautiful jewellery.

That was enough of a draw card, without the added promise:

> ...experienced readers can offer you insights and perspectives you may not have considered with Tarot cards.

Plus they sold 'an array of body products'!

Please don't think I'd suddenly lost faith in the all-round abilities of tea tree oil – that wouldn't happen for at least another few months – but I was curious to read that amongst candles and incense and oils, you could also purchase some 'smudge'. I had to get me some of this, although I wasn't too sure why. Perhaps it worked like Vaseline on a camera lens and just gave an overall softer (read 'younger') appearance. If that was the case, I was ready to toss any excess stuff out of the Winnebago to make room for several cases. After all, I hadn't been over-using the kitchen sink and stove!

Another draw card was the promise of healing massages from a well-trained therapist. You could choose from a 'soothing rub on the terrace' or 'the full experience in our heated room'. I was leaning towards the 'full experience' – and let's face it, who wouldn't – but I did wonder what it felt like to have your terrace rubbed. As we pulled over to the side of the road to consult the map, Hon did the navigational honours this time.

'It looks as though this place is up in the mountains. Are you still interested?' he asked.

I admit I had shown a slight nervous disposition the last time Winnie had traversed mountains, but was he seriously suggesting we bypass all this excitement just because of a few hills?

'It can't be that bad, can it?' I asked, ever the optimist. And this wonderful attraction was housed in a castle – a proper one this time, if the picture on the brochure was any indication – and proper castles were always built on mountains. I couldn't wait.

At the beginning of the journey, Winnie handled the gentle curves and slight ascension with ease, but as we ventured higher, the road became not only steeper but much narrower. I was aware of a nervous tic in my left cheek as we approached yet another sharp bend, and at one point, I threw my body towards the dashboard in the vain hope this would disperse weight and assist the van to progress up what resembled a sheer cliff face. One thing I was determined to do, however, was keep my cool. I wasn't giving Driver Dan a chance to utter those words 'I warned you', so gritted my teeth and hung on for dear life. But the road seemed endless, and after a particularly sharp curve, my self-control and I parted company.

'Pleeease, let's turn back,' I screamed.

'It's okay, we'll make it,' Hon said calmly.

He continued to slowly manoeuvre the van around the hairpin

bends, but this time I was silent. I was now sure any vibration inside the cabin would send the van careening over the edge. Actually, Driver Dan had already realised there was nowhere to turn around and we just had to keep going but how wise of him to wait until the next day before sharing this piece of information.

After what felt like three hours, but Hon assures me was twenty minutes, we finally arrived. The castle was nestled in a tropical rainforest and exuded a feeling of calm you could almost reach out and grab. We wandered up a path flanked with large boulders of crystals glinting in the muted sunlight shining through the dense foliage.

'I think the first thing we should do is book you in for a relaxing massage,' said my hero.

'Sounds great,' I said, unclenching my jaw.

The shop and café had been built around a central courtyard, and again there was an overwhelming feeling of peace and calm. Each of the employees seemed to wear mystical smiles, and when the waitress approached us for our orders I was tempted to say, 'I'll have what they're having.'

'All the staff probably live on the premises,' I said. 'No one could look that calm if they have to come up that road every day.'

After sitting in the forecourt listening to the musical calls of the tropical birds, it was soon time for my massage, and I was led up a spiral staircase to the turret of the castle, and almost expected to find a young girl sitting at a spinning wheel nursing an injured finger.

I was standing at the window when the door opened and a man in his early twenties entered. He had the face of an angel, with a clear unblemished complexion and pale blue eyes. Eyes this colour are often described as 'ice blue' and considered cold, but his were warm and welcoming. He wore a loose pair of cheesecloth pants and top and leather sandals, and his beautifully modulated voice completed the picture of serenity.

He gestured for me to take the seat opposite, and leaning forward, peered deeply into my eyes. 'Before we start, I like to know if there's one area of your body you'd like me to concentrate on.'

'Well, I do feel a bit tense around the neck and shoulders and down the back – and around the arms – and a bit on my legs. Oh, yes, and my head – it feels kind of – tight,' I replied, my voice a whisper by this stage.

A few moments passed, as he continued to look through me. 'Are you worried about anything in particular at the moment?' he finally asked.

'What, apart from the fact that I could be turning into a hypochondriac?' I nearly said.

'I am worried about going down the mountain again,' I finally admitted. 'The brochure said the drive would be breathtaking, but I didn't realise my breath would be taken in terror,' I said, laughing nervously.

He smiled politely at the lame humour. 'Let's see if we can ease a bit of that tension,' he said, as he invited me to hop up on the table and lie on my back. He moved to the corner of the room, and suddenly the haunting sounds of wooden pipes and the trickle of running water landing in what sounded like a bucket, filled the room.

Great! Now I had something else to worry about.

I'm constantly bewildered by the word 'menopause'. It doesn't even make sense. I can tell you, quite categorically, and with the expertise of experience, that there was no pause (not even the slightest hesitation) when I was thrust forward into the world of sweat-soaked hot flushes, skin which demanded a bucket, not just a jar of moisturiser, and calls of nature every half hour. And this final symptom rarely needed the encouragement of a gushing fountain!

With enormous powers of concentration, I blocked out the sound of Victoria Falls and felt my body relaxing. So much so I would not have been at all surprised to find myself levitating.

For the next hour, this man's fingers worked their magic, and I was transported to my own slice of heaven. The world was in slow motion, and I was seriously contemplating joining a silent order of nuns who live at this pace every day.

Finally my 'angel' stood back from the table, and placed a gentle hand on my shoulder. 'I'll just leave you to come around in your own time. I'll be waiting downstairs.'

The door quietly opened, and he disappeared.

It took every bit of willpower to leave piping Pan and his piddling pail. I was lying on powdery white sand trailing my toes in the warm crystal waters of a Tahitian lagoon. But remembering my appointment with the fortune teller, I forced myself to step from the table, and leave the room.

The 'magic-fingered one' was waiting at the bottom of the stairs. 'Just follow me and I'll show you where to go for your reading,' he said.

We climbed the staircase once again, but just before reaching the top, he ushered me through a small alcove.

'Please take a seat. She'll be with you in a moment.'

Just as he turned to leave, I couldn't resist one last comment. 'Thank you again, that was wonderful,' I said. 'Any chance we can give you a ride down the mountain? I'll probably need another massage by the time we hit the plains.'

I'm sure he thought I was joking, as he just gave another beautiful smile and left the room.

Before I had too much time to take in my surroundings, a woman of indeterminate age and piercing eyes walked into the room and introduced herself.

The European accent was thick as butter as she handed me a pack of tired-looking Tarot cards. 'Pliss – you shovel cardz,' she said.

I could understand the reference to a 'spade' – the cards were twice the size of a normal deck. I must have been extremely relaxed from the massage because as soon as I started to 'shovel', the entire deck headed to the four corners of the room. After clambering round the floor, I handed the pack back.

She spread the cards in a semi circle and pointed. 'Four cardz – pliss pick.'

Pick – shovel – the woman had a gardening fetish! I held my fingers over the cards until I experienced the familiar tingling which usually guided my selection.

She sat motionless for several minutes, studying the cards I had chosen. 'You are creatif pipple – not doink enuff.' Her dark eyes penetrated mine. 'Must giffink up verk you are doink now – write more – much happy – much excess in two, mebby three year.'

Excess? Maybe she meant 'success'. Yes, I liked that.

She went on to talk about other aspects of my life, but I wasn't listening. I was going to be successful, so everything else would fall into place.

As we reached the end of the reading, she looked up. 'Do you huff any kvestions you are nidding to usk?'

I smiled and shook my head. I had heard all I needed to, and it was a more relaxed navigator who hopped into the passenger seat half an hour later. The gentle fingers of the masseuse had worked their magic on my tense body and even the aura of peace and calm had penetrated every pore. And yes, I could even imagine my terrace felt better!

But there was also another significant reason for my relaxed demeanour. My gypsy forecaster had stilled my troubled mind when she predicted I would have success with my writing in two to three years' time. This meant just one thing. I wasn't going to die going down the mountain!

14

A few years ago, I sat in a darkened theatre waiting for the curtain to rise on *Phantom of the Opera*, about to realise one of the dreams on my current wish list. I knew the music backwards and was about to be drawn into the world of this beautiful love story. I sat entranced as the gondola made its way slowly across the stage and the masked phantom serenaded Christine.

But a few hours later I felt enormous disappointment. Not at the production; it was everything I had imagined and more. But I had just realised one of my dreams and it could now be crossed off the list. As much as I hated to admit it, half the excitement of a dream is the anticipation; the longer we have the dream, the more heightened the expectations. And this is what happened with Byron Bay!

I had wanted to see this coastal town in New South Wales for years; the place where the flower children of the seventies rubbed shoulders with the upwardly mobile of the 'noughties', where the sun shone constantly on a laid-back lifestyle in beautiful beach-side surroundings. And it looked promising as we drove down the main street and saw the footpaths bustling with an eclectic bunch of people. Dreadlocked youths manoeuvred their surfboards over the heads of casual strollers, and the smell of board wax mingled with the cloying aroma of hash.

The caravan park was in the main street and, as we drove through the rows of vans, it became obvious space was at a premium. Our allotment was a piece of lawn only fractionally larger than our nature strip back home. For once, Driver Dan agreed some navigational help would be required, but we had this task down to a fine art by now, and in a few minutes our craft was nestled on its green strip.

On several occasions this had proved an irresistible piece of entertainment for other park residents, and we even received a round of applause from one group after a hair-raising but successful reversing procedure. But when I smiled at the family next door and received a cool glare in return, I realised things were different down Byron way.

There was hardly enough room to set up our usual alfresco dining area of one small table and two foldaway chairs. At least we had been given beach-front accommodation, and this afforded us an uninterrupted view of the Pacific Ocean. But I was anxious to immerse myself in my dream, so leaving Hon to have his post-drive drink, I headed for the main street. The 'doof doof' music coming from the beer garden of the hotel clashed with the mystical Indian sitars drifting from the New Age shops, and nut-brown teenagers with outfits the size of a cocktail napkin, yelled at each other across the street.

When we knew Byron Bay would be on the itinerary, I was determined to buy some bathers from this trendy place. But as I walked into one of the boutiques and shared this information with the slim, young shop assistant, she appraised me for several seconds, and frowned.

'Yeah,' she sighed. 'Look, I think you're gonna need a high-cut leg – give you more length – know what I mean?' she said.

How simple – why hadn't that dawned on me before? All those years when I was desperate for a few more inches!

'Okay,' I said, taking a deep breath before continuing. 'But let me ask you one thing. Do you honestly think a large flab of hip and buttocks hanging out of my bathers would seriously be considered part of my leg?'

I could only assume the hours she had spent in the sun to obtain skin the colour of boot polish had affected her brain. She raised what was left of a heavily plucked eyebrow, gave me a second glance and sighed. I was going to be her challenge for the day.

Her eyes slowly travelled up my body, finally settling in the region of my chest. 'What size are you – in the boobs, like?'

'I'm a 12E,' I said, pleased she had given up on the arse end of the bathers.

'Did you say E?' She couldn't have sounded more incredulous had I announced I possessed a third mammary gland. 'Er – I don't think we go that big.'

She paused, and I hoped she was looking for an answer to this problem – but no. 'We sell heaps of – like – Bs.'

I wasn't sure what reaction she expected, but my mind was busy with a rather frightening visual. It seemed the only bathers on offer would expose so much of my arse and boobs I'd be left with just enough material for a rather thin belt. And let's not even start on my stomach!

After she flicked through every hanger in the shop, she finally produced three pairs of bathers with a D cup. I rushed to the fitting room, but privacy was not a priority in this fashion hellhole. The two swing doors took their job seriously and were destined never to meet. I had just dropped my shorts and was bending over about to step into Exhibit A, when wooden slats bashed against my rump.

'How's it going?' our anorexic assistant chirped. 'Any of them fit?'

'Maybe a two-year-old,' I nearly chirped back. 'I'll call you if I need any assistance,' I said, indicating she should probably leave if she valued her life, and acknowledging I'd just morphed into my mother at her haughtiest! I did entertain the idea of asking for a shoehorn for the excess flesh, but doubted our young friend would know what I was talking about.

It will come as no surprise that I left the shop ten minutes later without making a purchase.

Once more I became one with the seething masses, my feet hardly touching the ground as I was carried along. When I noticed a middle-aged man sitting on a small woven rug on the footpath next to a sign advertising 'Henna Tattoos', I managed to disentangle myself from the masses. He was dressed in a tired T-shirt and sarong that had seen better days – probably round the dawning of the age of Aquarius – and his dreads were grey.

I had recently been sent into a state of near hysteria necessitating a shot of Valium when my eldest son had proudly displayed a tattoo of a large bird of prey on his upper right arm. Perhaps it was time to extract my revenge!

'How much for a dolphin?' I asked.

The man sneered at me through his dirt encrusted ringlets. 'Fifteen dollars for you.'

I was struggling to work out whether this was a bargain. Was that pensioner discount, or was he charging more in case the colour seeped into the wrinkles and extra ink was required?

'How long do they last?' We were due home in three weeks; I wouldn't bother having one if it was going to fade in two.

'Trying to impress the kids, are we?' Bob Marley said, giving a derisive snort. 'Show them how trendy we are?' He shook his head, and there was even sarcasm in his smile.

Suddenly I saw red. 'That's ripe, coming from someone like you. At least I'm living in the present, mate, not desperately clutching on to an image that worked for me back in the seventies.' I gave him what I hoped was a look of steel, my version of a derisive snort, and walked off down the street, my head held high. My body, like John West, would remain dolphin-safe.

For dinner that night we decided to indulge in some local seafood. Sitting at an outdoor restaurant, I was watching the passing people parade when I spotted a young guy who not only had a successful recording career in this country but also had made several films both here and in America. As I caught his eye, I smiled in acknowledgement, and he made a beeline for our table.

'How's it going?' he asked, and I was surprised to see how chuffed he was at being recognised.

'Good,' I said. 'What brings you to Byron?'

'We're doing a gig at the pub tonight – why don't you come along?'

His two friends, who I assumed were band members, turned and looked at him, their jaws making a loud clunk as they hit the pavement.

I wouldn't have minded seeing the band live – they had a good sound and a good reputation – but suddenly I was transported back to the sixties. I was fifteen and waiting for the Beatles to come on stage at their Melbourne concert when I noticed a woman my mother's age a few rows in front of me.

I nudged my girlfriend. 'Somebody better tell her Frank Sinatra's not on tonight.'

We both collapsed at my rapier wit, but the message was clear. There is an unwritten rule; the generations do not encroach on each other's territory.

I smiled at the young singer. 'We'll see – but thanks for the invite anyway.'

What a nice guy. He was the only one out of the three who looked genuinely disappointed.

A few mornings later, I was sitting outside the van having my first cup of tea. It was still early, about five-thirty, but I found it almost impossible to sleep any later in Byron. A stretch of sand was the only thing separating us from the Pacific Ocean, and the sound of the crashing surf penetrated Winnie's walls very effectively.

I wasn't the only one awake in the Bay, however. My entertainment was guaranteed as I watched the surfers who had been lured out of their sleeping bags on the beach with the promise of that one special wave. And if the sound of the ocean hadn't been so loud, I probably would have heard, before I saw, the young couple on the beach in front of our van, professing their lust for each other in a succession of groans resembling lions at feeding time.

'What are we still doing here?' I thought. We weren't due to leave till the next day, but I'd certainly seen enough. Hon didn't take much convincing when he woke a few hours later, and we didn't even stop for breakfast.

A few months after arriving home, I came across a documentary on the dolphin population of Byron Bay. They were saying researchers had counted up to eight hundred dolphins in the area, with a constant group of approximately twenty females and babies. The matriarch of the group, who had been named Fingers (no, they didn't say why), looked after them all, and if an aggressive pod of male dolphins approached the group, she would slap her tail against the surface of the water, to direct the other females to stay close by.

What a great story, I thought, but possibly pure fiction. What dolphin in their right mind would hang around such a place? And with seven hundred and ninety-nine others? It wasn't only the footpaths of Byron that were crowded. And why would they choose to swim in the same waters as the great-unwashed dreadlocked surfers? No, I graced them with far more intelligence than that. I never once saw a hint of a fin when I was gazing across the ocean each morning at 'Claustrophobia Cove'. And as we left that day, we both agreed that sometimes the anticipation of dreams is often better than the realisation.

15

Although we were less than a hundred kilometres from Tweed Heads and Coolangatta, the sunshine playgrounds of southern Queensland, we wanted to concentrate on coastal New South Wales, so it was time to head south.

The drive between Byron Bay and Grafton was picturesque, as the scenery drifted from lush green forests to tropical cane fields. Grafton is situated on the Clarence River, forty kilometres from the coast, and the wide streets complemented the elegant Victorian buildings. The original owners of these places probably made their money through dairy farming or sugar cane plantations, two industries that still sustain the district.

Having missed breakfast in Byron and not even stopping for coffee, we were more than ready for a break at Grafton. Although there were at least twenty restaurants and cafés listed in the Grafton literature, we had our hearts set on hamburger and fries. When we drove into the local McDonalds, it was still fairly early for the lunch crowd, and the car park was almost empty. But half an hour later when our appetite was appeased, it was a different story. We could only assume this was a popular lunch spot for Graftonians, and Winnie was surrounded.

I shouldn't have been surprised how easily Driver Dan had taken to handling our gal Winnie. He never seemed to have a problem handling me and, if the men throughout my life could be believed, this was no easy task! You could almost see the smile on Winnie's grill as we sailed along the highways, and when he showed confidence in her ability to climb every mountain and ford every stream, Winnie came through.

But was his easy relationship with Win about to change? This time it appeared he'd backed his girl into a tight spot, and no woman likes that feeling.

'I think you'll have to guide me out,' Hon said. 'I haven't got much room to negotiate.'

I stood behind, and slightly to the right of the van, and beckoned Driver Dan, but there was hardly any room. 'Stop – that's as far as you can go!' I yelled.

A Toyota Echo parked behind had almost joined us permanently for the rest of the holiday. Running round to the front of the van, I beckoned Hon towards me. He put the Winnie into gear and started to creep forward.

'That's it,' I yelled again. 'You've only got an inch left before you hit the Magna.' I was too stressed for metric.

This toing and froing went on for another five minutes, until Driver Dan switched off the engine and stuck his head out of the window. 'Nup, it's not going to work. We'll just wait till the owner of one of these cars comes back from lunch.'

Here is yet another example of my man's infinite patience and my – let me see, how shall I put it – my haste to get things done sooner rather than later.

'How do you know the drivers are even in Maccers?' I asked. 'No, I'm going to ask the staff to make an announcement.'

But this suggestion was not met with the enthusiasm I was expecting. 'You can't do that. It's not as if they're parked illegally. No, let's just wait. I'm sure they won't be too long.'

Just as the steam started escaping from my ears, a man walked over to the Magna, hopped in and drove off. Smug doesn't really cover the look sent my way!

It must have been the demands on my navigational abilities, or maybe the double cheeseburger, large fries and shake which sent me into a deep sleep soon after we cleared the Grafton suburbs, but the next thing Hon was shaking me.

'Wake up, babe. You don't want to miss this.'

I thought I'd seen the ultimate in fibreglass fruit when I stood next to the Big Orange, which is located just outside the town of Berri in South Australia, and now I was confronted with another. But this one was yellow and, so I learned later, was your ferro-concrete, not your fibreglass.

The Big Banana was built in 1964, and we have an American by the name of John Landi to thank for the first giant Australian man-made landmark. John originally came to Australia to study the insects attacking the commercial banana plantations. He opened a milk bar specialising in banana milk shakes and, copying the Big Pineapple in Hawaii, came up with his own promotion.

As a toddler, one of my sons had difficulty pronouncing this particular fruit, and this was a source of amusement to the local Italian greengrocer.

'Hey, little man, whatcha calla these things, eh?' Connie would ask, throwing a wink in my direction. 'Buggers,' was the response, and it never failed to have the desired effect, as Connie wiped the tears from her eyes with her apron.

At eleven metres long, five metres high and 2.4 metres wide, I was looking at one of the biggest buggers I'd ever seen!

We climbed the elevated walkway to the Coffs Coast Lookout and took in spectacular views of the area. But even though we were there at the right time of the year, we didn't 'witness the migration of the whales', as the brochure promised.

The souvenir shop had provided the local artisans an outlet for their creativity regarding bananas. Remembering my blow-out at a certain 'castle of nuts', I managed to control my spending. Besides, yellow did absolutely nothing for the décor back home. Instead, I concentrated on learning some more about the world's largest herb. I couldn't help picking up on a common theme at these tourist places where the local product was being promoted. Apparently if you purchased kilograms, gallons, litres or pounds of whatever they were trying to sell, it would cure any medical condition known to mankind.

I had already been given 'the good oil' about the tea tree, but it seemed the humble banana was also quite capable of holding its own. Although there were bananas which had been dried, chipped, jammed, chutneyed, pickled, split and choc-coated, I was more impressed with what it could achieve in its natural form. This fruit was capable of eliminating blood pressure, constipation, depression, hangovers, heartburn, morning sickness and PMS. And expectant mothers in Thailand even eat bananas to ensure that their babies are born with a cool temperature. Must admit I didn't know this was important! And don't waste time seeing your doctor about warts. Just place a banana skin on top, secure it with surgical tape, and *voilà*, no more wart!

As we wandered out of the shop clutching our bag of 'wonder drugs', there was one more thing I needed to do before we left, so the camera was dragged from the bag.

Now there's an unusual phenomenon that happens with these super-size structures. Without exception, in real life they all seem a trifle tired-looking, could do with a new paint job, and are nowhere near as big as you imagined. But you still need a photo of it, and just as well. Because when you pick up your developed film from the chemist shop, something miraculous has happened. The prawn or gumboot or orange or banana looks fantastic. The camera has smoothed out the flaws which were so obvious in real life, and you are positively dwarfed by this structure you thought was a lot smaller in reality.

I fell in love with Coffs Harbour. There could have been a number of reasons, but it started the minute we settled in at the Park Beach Caravan Park. Although the park was nearly full, we had a wonderful feeling of space around us. Situated on a popular surf beach and still only five minutes to the city centre, there was clear water and white sands on one side, and Coffs Creek abutting a shaded picnic area on the other. And the people actually smiled and talked to you!

We had only just reached step two in our arrival checklist, when a young father approached us.

'Nice-looking van,' he said.

Clinging to his leg was the cutest little girl with wisps of strawberry-blonde curls, almost enough freckles to join into a suntan, and long lashed hazel/green eyes. A smaller version was gazing at me from a baby sling strung across Dad's chest.

Each park we stayed in, there always seemed to be someone who was fascinated by the size and facilities the Winnebago offered, so I became quite adept at hosting what I dubbed 'Mini Winnie Wanders' to show our girl off.

'Thanks. Would you like to have a look inside?' I said.

I had this 'tour' thing down pat. To enable our 'guest' to gain an overall perspective of the accommodation provided, I would stand in the centre of the van, and indicate the different areas, with arm movements any Qantas flight attendant would have envied. But I had only just started on my super spiel, when the young father interrupted.

'How many litres per hundred ks does this give you?'

I did a rapid search of my memory bank, but couldn't find an answer. 'I'm not sure – my husband would probably know.' I was desperate to get back on to familiar territory. 'Anyway, you can see how much storage space is provided, something you'd need with these little ones,' I said, smiling at the poppets who seemed mesmerised by my rapid arm movements.

'What's the freshwater capacity compared to the grey water?'

Grey water? Was he talking about Winnie the Poo, because 'grey' is hardly the description I would have chosen.

'Er, I'm not sure of the exact capacity, but I think we have a brochure I could find and let you know.' I indicated the sofa. 'This can be used as a bed as well – handy that.'

He gave it a cursory glance, but his mind was elsewhere. 'I assume the fridge runs on gas when you're away from power?'

At last! A question I could answer. 'Yes, that's one of the things you must do the minute you arrive, and just before you leave – switch over.' I paused. 'We have quite a comprehensive checklist.' I was sure this would impress him, but he'd heard enough.

'Yes, well, thanks for the look – I'll just have a quick word with your husband on the way out.'

Most people, however, were just interested in looking around inside. After a standard-size caravan, the 'bago must have looked enormous, and their questions were always within the comfort zone of my knowledge.

As we sat with our pre-dinner drinks and enjoying the activity around the park one night, I noticed a man standing next to a small, tired-looking caravan parked two lots away. He was staring in our direction.

'Minnie Winnie Wander tour number seven coming up,' I muttered into my brandy.

Sure enough, the man casually stuck his hands into his trouser pockets and ambled our way. 'See you're from South Australia too,' he said. 'They hard to manoeuvre?' he asked, nodding Winnie's way.

'Not bad,' Driver Dan said. 'You soon get used to it.'

I stood up. 'Would you like a look inside?'

He peered towards the entrance, and sucked air through his teeth. 'Nup, not really. Just wondered what part of SA you're from.'

I told him the suburb, but must admit feeling a little deflated. Until that moment I hadn't acknowledged the almost maternal pride I'd taken in our gal Win, and almost forgot we had only fostered her for a short time, not adopted for the long haul.

The man stared at me, his eyes narrowing as he scratched vigorously at the multicoloured chin stubble. 'Get outta here. You couldn't live there. You're having me on!'

Well, yes, we could live there, and we did. And I wasn't about to 'have him on' anything! Did he know something about this suburb we didn't? Maybe while we were travelling, there had been an earthquake, and just this part of Adelaide had been razed. But surely we would have heard?

'Which street are you in?' His question dragged me back to the present.

I told him, and as he threw his head back, the crackle of a phlegm-laden cough revealed a possible pack-a-day habit.

He ran his hands through the few grey hairs still clinging desperately to his liver-spotted scalp. 'I'm just round the bleeding corner!' This was obviously too much excitement for one day, as the cough turned into a deep wheeze, and his face took on the colour of a satsuma plum.

I was about to offer him a glass of water when the coughing stopped as suddenly as it had started.

'Listen,' he said, surveying us through watery eyes, and pointing to our drinks, 'I don't want to stop you good people from having your afternoon tipple. How's about I go and grab a beer and join you?'

How could we refuse? He now knew where we lived. If we said 'No', could he stalk us when we arrived home? Within a few minutes he was back, carrying a can of Toohey's and an outdoor chair with dangerously thin webbing.

'Best drink of the day,' he said, plonking himself down with a little too much exuberance, but thankfully the chair held. 'Just been given the boot at work, so my mate told me to take his van and just get lost for a while. First driving holiday I've had in years. Worked for an airline back in the late sixties and seventies – you wouldn't believe how cheap the fares were with your staff discount – and when I left, I was hooked on flying holidays.'

I smiled. 'I know what you mean. I worked for Ansett back then, and took advantage of the fares as well.'

'Bloody hell, I don't believe it.' Beer splashed from the can, as the man sat forward in his chair, and slapped me on the knee. 'That's the airline I worked for!' His eyes creased as he stared at me. 'Don't remember you, though, love. Were you flight crew?'

'No, I worked in admin, first in the Melbourne office then I was transferred to Adelaide.'

We spent the next ten minutes throwing names at each other, marvelling at how small Australia can be. He now felt comfortable enough to regale us with all of his employment history, and there was one more coincidence before our friend emptied his can and folded up his chair.

'I worked for the Electricity Trust of South Australia in the early eighties. That wasn't a bad job – made some good friends. One of my ETSA mates lent me the van.'

And now it was Hon's turn to be amazed. 'I worked for them in the early eighties,' he said and, after comparing dates, found they'd missed each other by a few months!

I've often wondered if our 'local friend' dined out on that story when he arrived back home – I know we did.

Maybe my love affair with Coffs Harbour had something to do with the fact that the area had the best climate in Australia, with maximum temperatures rarely falling below 19°C summer or winter. You've got to love a place like that. And how it was named as well! Captain John Korff originally discovered it when he was looking for a safe port in a storm. He named the place Korff's Harbour, but the misspelling occurred when it was gazetted later.

The first day in Korff's 'Arbour, we woke to one of those perfect days, with the temperature already at 25C, with the promise of a maximum 28C and afternoon sea breezes. After a morning swim, we headed off to the Pet Porpoise Pool, a local attraction for the past twenty-eight years in Korff's. The brochure promised 'an interactive sea circus display for people who want to do more than just watch marine mammals in action' and I was definitely that 'people'.

We ate our lunch in the picnic grounds of the complex where many of the injured or orphaned animals were being rehabilitated. The staff work closely with the National Parks and Wildlife Service and provide a recovery refuge for stranded or injured marine life as well. The dolphin pools are built as a raised construction with the water level at waist height, so we were able to pat and play catch with the dolphins. Stroking their rubbery skin and looking into their intelligent eyes, I wondered just who was entertaining who.

The sea circus display occupied us for the next hour and a half and was everything they had promised. I was thrilled with the interactive part as I stood on the edge of a high platform dangling a fish over the pool, and laughed as the dolphin shot out of the water and grabbed it. And you haven't lived till you've been smooched by a seal and played ball with a dolphin!

It wasn't until we left Coffs Harbour that I read in the brochure there are only dolphins, not porpoises, at the Pet Porpoise Pool. Perhaps alliteration was too difficult with the letter D!

16

The day we were due to leave Korff's, we both emerged from the van just as the sun was easing over the horizon.

'May as well get an early start,' Hon said. 'I'll start breakfast while you have a shower.'

Heading for the ablution block, I noticed it was so early hardly anyone else was about so, ignoring my conscience about water conservation, I took an extra long shower. I had just finished dressing and was plugging in the hair dryer when the door flew open and a young girl walked in. She looked no older than fifteen and was carrying a large striped shopping bag which she dumped on the floor. This would usually be an irresistible scenario for me. I have always been curious – some would say nosy – about people and their stories, and often engage strangers in conversation if I think they look interesting. But this time I managed to curb my enthusiasm. Hon was intent on an early start, so I sprayed my hair with root lifter, and remained mute.

'Hi.'

I turned and smiled at the young girl. 'Hello. Looks like we're the only ones mad enough to be up at this hour. Are you heading off this morning as well?' Why do I do that? Ask a question I know will extend the conversation when I want to get away.

'No,' she said, shaking her head as she leant against the cubicle door. 'This is the only way I can get any peace. The walls of the van start closing in on me, and I just need a break before the day starts going insane.' She gave me a smile which was already tired. 'And today's going to be extra crazy.'

Picking up the bag, she walked over to the bench and tipped out the contents. Packets of multicoloured balloons, rolls of streamers, several packets of toys and wrapping paper spilt onto the floor. 'It's my son's fourth birthday and I want to get this lot organised before he wakes up.'

I took a closer look at the long brown hair framing the small oval face dominated by soulful, dark eyes. Her complexion was flawless and, even when she threw a smile in my direction, her face maintained the smooth blank canvas of youth.

'You don't look old enough to have a child,' I said, finding it hard to disguise my astonishment.

'Yeah, I know.' She shrugged. 'People are always telling me that. I've got two others – a boy two and a little girl six months.'

The thought of travelling in a cramped caravan with such a young baby was bad enough, but to add a 'terrible two' and a 'kindergarten kamikaze' to the mix was asking for trouble.

'You must have a large van to accommodate that lot.'

'Not really,' she said, ripping open one of the packets and pulling out a bright yellow balloon. 'We've got an annexe we attach to the van, but we've had to leave that for my husband's parents.'

My God, was she part of Wirth's Circus? The early morning departure was fast losing its attraction – I was hooked and had to know more.

I walked over to the bench, sat down and took a balloon from the packet. 'Are you planning to blow up all of these?' I asked.

'Probably – I want to give the little man a surprise when he wakes up. I'm going to hang them all over the van, and some outside as well.'

We worked quietly together until the floor round our feet was covered in a rainbow of rubber, and there were enough balloons to satisfy not only one, but all three children.

I leant back and glanced at the young mother. 'I can just imagine how stressful it would be travelling in a caravan with three children, but to include your in-laws as well – the mind boggles. How long have you been on the road?'

She grabbed a ball of string and cutting it into small lengths attached them to each balloon knot. 'Only nine months – but it seems like forever.'

Nine months! Hang on, arithmetic was never my strong point, but I didn't need a calculator this time. 'Didn't you say you had a six-month-old?'

'Yes, she's beautiful.' The smile transformed her face. 'That's why we brought Jason's folks with us. My mother-in-law helped with the birth, and my father-in-law kept the other two out of mischief while I was busy.'

I had never heard the process of childbirth put in such simple terms. This tiny little thing was truly a modern-day pioneer.

'Anyway, I want my kids to be surrounded by love. I grew up in foster homes, and I know how important a family is.'

While we were talking, she had gathered the balloons into bunches and wrapped the presents in Wiggles paper. We walked out of the ablution block, both laden with party paraphernalia, and when we reached her van, I placed my armful onto an outdoor chair.

'Thanks for your help – it was really kind of you,' she said, smiling shyly.

I reached forward and wrapped my arms around her small frame. 'No – thank you. You're a remarkable girl. Those kids of yours are very lucky to have such a wonderful mother.'

'That little town we're supposed to check out is only eight kilometres south,' I said, gazing at the map as we headed 'orff from Korff's'. When we discussed our itinerary with friends, several mentioned Sawtell and said it was well worth a visit. Not only was it popular for its beaches with great fishing, but also boasted an excellent shopping centre with a very pretty main street.

An outdoor café under a giant fig tree was the perfect place to have our morning coffee in the ambience of this quaint township with the village atmosphere. But we had only just sat down when my attention was drawn to the table next to us, where two middle-aged couples were having a heated discussion in German. It has always been a regret of mine that I am not bilingual, but in this case it didn't matter. From the body language and tone of the words, there was no doubt a disagreement was taking place.

The two males were poring over a large two-ring binder packed with not only brochures, but also printouts from the Internet. The folder was divided into sections and, much to my delight, the dividers were written in both German and English. I nonchalantly moved my chair closer to their table under the pretence of avoiding the sun, and glanced at the section headings. Were all men the same? The folder was divided into 'Waterfalls', 'Lighthouses', 'Lookouts', 'Golf Courses', et cetera, and I knew if we stayed there long enough, a 'Blowhole' section would be revealed!

When the husbands both pointed at the brochure highlighting the two headland lookouts close by, the wives' look of disdain surpassed the language barrier. The girls had their own brochure and this one extolled the virtues of Sawtell and its excellent shopping centre. The only thing these two girls were on the lookout for were bargains! We didn't have time to wait around and see who won, but I'd put my money on the wives.

I turned to see if Hon had been aware of the drama at the table next door, but he was smiling at something else.

Thrusting the menu in my direction, he pointed to item number four, 'carrot pecan current (sic) orange bread'. 'Saves time, I guess, and that way they cater for all tastes,' he said.

During our trip, we had commented on the number of misspellings in menus, and started making note of these in, you guessed it, a list – this particular one had the heading 'Fractured Food'.

One of the items already on our list was a similar 'all-in-one'. This café offered 'muesli/cappacino/latte in a mug with cookie' and we thought this a wonderful idea, albeit a trifle messy, for the traveller in a hurry. We were tempted to indulge but settled for the 'fresh expresso', hoping this would make us more articulate after consumption?

Another of my favourites was 'ravoli with spagettie sauce', and I felt it safe to assume the proprietor was not Italian!

We've all heard stories about the vengeful acts some chefs perform when a diner complains about the meal. But isn't serving 'leak and onion soup' carrying things a bit too far?

And the lists didn't stop there. Signs along the roadside kept catching my eye, and although a lot were misspelled as well, this next list bore the heading 'Peculiar Pairs'. I seriously doubt whether I would ever have come up with these combinations in my wildest dreams!

'Turkish handmade carpets and smoked eels'. Was this a suggestion that when shopping for floor coverings you should take your time and even combine it with an afternoon snack?

'Worms and Wombats Tourist Attraction'. Hopefully they were kept in separate accommodation. I know a wombat eats roots and leaves, but I'm sure they're not averse to the occasional worm.

'Farm Cleanups – lizards and tortoises'. Admittedly I'm a city girl, but I didn't think these particular animals were in plague proportions on a farm. Or maybe they use lizards and tortoises to clean up other animals.

'Furniture made to order – enquire at ice creamery'. A recliner in gelato colours, perhaps?

'Cow Lotto and Fete'. I wanted to ask if they home delivered first prize, but Hon refused to pull over.

But the lengthiest list of all was the one headed 'Baarstard Inglish'.

'Please keep of garden' had us wondering which part of garden would they like us to keep.

'Come in and see our Great Souvenire' and we were tempted. After all, it was so great, they only needed one, and had even made it into a proper noun. Pity about the improper spelling!

'One pear of purple beeds' (this was written on our receipt). One look at the shop assistant and I just knew 'amethyst necklace' would be beyond her.

'Funky tye died fashions'. Deceased since the seventies! Wanted to recommend the young shop owner allow her mother to proofread advertising signs.

And the last list of all – 'Questions Without Answers.' Although I was determined to keep us amused during the many hours of travel, there were occasions when music, cryptic crosswords, news items from the local paper and attractions of the next town failed to hold my interest, and with my head leant against the window gazing at the passing scenery, my mind was filled with questions.

Why do cows in a paddock all face the same way? Is there a leader of the pack who decides the direction first thing in the morning?

Why do cement water towers have windows? Who's looking out?

What do you do on a Wind Farm Tour? And what do they sell in the souvenir shop?

Do Tidy Towns win anything apart from the sign which announces they are?

How come the 'trust' system in rural Australia works but is never seen in the cities? You know, the signs on the fruit and vegetable stalls saying '1kg bag of apples for sale – please leave money in the tin'. The same applies to the small rural golf courses and their green fees.

Why was there a sign in the middle of nowhere that read 'Drive on left in Australia'? How did foreigners reach this point without knowing that?

Why do fellow campervan drivers give each other the one-fingered (index, not middle) salute? Are we now a member of a secret organisation?

I never did find answers to these questions, but I decided to address the 'campervan salute' issue with my own version.

Although there are numerous campervans and caravans on the highways of Australia, you don't see many Winnebagos. I became so excited when we spotted one, I felt it deserved its own special salute. This necessitated holding the index and middle finger of each hand in a V, bringing the hands together, and *voilà* – you have a W. And from the looks on our fellow Winnie Wanderers, I could only assume they were amazed at this stroke of genius!

17

The town of Kempsey was such a surprise. I had no idea it was on the coast. I didn't really know much about it at all, except for one fact that has never come up in any trivia quiz I have seen.

A boy called David Kirkpatrick was born in Kempsey back in 1940, and at the age of ten changed his name to Slim Dusty and became Australia's most famous country singer. Somehow country singers should be brought up in the outback, amongst the dust and flies, not in a mid-north coastal town located on the Macleay River, halfway between Sydney and the Queensland border.

We scanned the local literature to see if there was anything we should check out. I'm sure the people of Kempsey are very proud of their town, and so they should be. But the only thing that attracted my attention was the information that Akubra, one of the most famous and distinctly Australian products, established their hat factory in the town in 1974.

Perhaps if we pass through again, I may suggest we stay at least one night – at the Mesopotamia Deer Park. With a name like that, there has to be a fascinating story attached. But this time, we were just happy to get back on the road, and head for our next destination.

Most of our overnights were just that, as it always came back to the mathematics. Not enough vacation time, divided by too many kilometres, multiplied by places we couldn't drag ourselves away from. Spreadsheet says 'No'. But when we were poring over the map in the early stages of planning, we did agree that some places required more than just one night. And the minute we drove into Port Macquarie, we had a good feeling about the planned three-day stopover.

The brochures call it 'a water lover's paradise' and they're right. Situated at the mouth of the Hastings River and the Pacific Ocean, there are no less than fifteen beaches within easy reach. For a town of forty thousand people, it has a wonderfully uncrowded feel to it and the Sundowner Breakwall Tourist Park proved to be idyllic, with a short walk to the beach one way, and a few minutes to the town centre in the other direction.

This is the part where I'm supposed to regale you with all the tourist spots we checked out, and point out there is so much to do in this great place. And there is – but we didn't. The surfing, rainforests, wildlife and nature parks, museums, walking trails and parklands sounded wonderful, but as we threw our towels down on the pristine sand and soaked up the warm sun, this little black duck and drake weren't going anywhere. We were suffering a case of tourist overload.

But when we did drag ourselves away from some holiday reading, the one place we headed was the twenty-seven-hole mini golf course. Now Hon is quite a good golfer, and although he's extremely modest, and would be quick to say 'Depends which day you're talking about', I only need to glance at the shelf above the computer to see a 'hole in one' trophy he received when he was a callow youth of fifteen.

Can't say the same for myself, however. As a golfer, I'm a great dancer, so although it seems less than modest, I can't help sharing this piece of information with you. I beat Hon at mini golf! Yes, all right, it's not like a real game, and it was by only one stroke, but from that moment on, I referred to myself as Princess Putt Putt of the Port.

He did redeem himself somewhat at the Hydro Golf, a rather unique idea where you try and hit targets in the middle of the lake, and if successful, collect the jackpot – sixty-four dollars that particular day. No, there was no jackpot collected, but he came so close, he was even drawing gasps of admiration from the other 'swingers'.

That night, to celebrate my wonderful victory, we lashed out at Crays Waterfront Restaurant and ordered lobster (mine mornay, his thermidor) and wandered back along the seafront to the caravan park. A perfect day, and just what we needed – a port in the storm of touring.

It depends who you believe about the naming of Lemon Tree Passage, part of the Tilligerry Peninsula on the northern shores of Port Stephens. The most obvious would be because of the lemon trees found growing by early settlers. Others say there is a native plant called cheese bush in the area, and this resembles a lemon tree. But why not call it 'Cheese Bush Passage'? That would make more sense. Personally I prefer the original name Kooindah, which means 'clear water'. That one says it all.

The area is well known for its colony of wild koalas, but they must have all been asleep that day. What was more exciting than a grey bundle of fluff snoring up a gum tree was the frenetic activity of the 'pelican feeding' which happens every day at the marina around one p.m. I could have sat on the beach and watched those magnificent birds all day, but our next stop beckoned.

Nelson Bay is only forty-one kilometres from Lemon Tree Passage, so we were soon settled at the Halifax Holiday Park. Although it wasn't as central to the main part of town as we were led to believe, we couldn't fault the location for its accessibility to the shores of two beaches.

At this stage of the holiday, our arrival checklist took exactly three and a half minutes, so four minutes later we were making our way through the bush walkway that led to a totally unspoilt beach. We spent the rest of the day wandering along the beach, checking out Shoal Haven, another holiday resort in the same area as Nelson Bay, and meandering back at dusk.

So much of our time this holiday was spent sitting in the van getting from point A to point B, we grabbed any opportunity for exercise. But this day I think we overdid it, as I was so exhausted the thought of cooking dinner in the van almost made me hyperventilate. Luckily, Nelson Bay had a bowling club!

When we checked the local map, we realised it was too far to walk to the club, so we called a taxi. A wiser woman would have read the signs or at least heard the warning bells, because when I mentioned pick-up would be from the caravan park, the booking bloke didn't even try for subtlety.

'The driver doesn't have time to wander round the whole bleedin' park lookin' for his fare, lady.'

I was tempted to point out that we were the sole Winnebago in the park, and therefore stood out like the dog's proverbials, but as they appeared to be the only taxi in town, I bit my tongue. We offered to wait by the entrance, and began to regret this when it started raining and the taxi was fifteen minutes late. We were just wondering whether to go back to the van and change into warmer clothes when there was a squeal of brakes and a spray of water.

'Didn't realise how cold it can get around here at night,' I said to the driver, as we slid in the back seat. 'At least the taxi's warm.'

The figure in the front seat remained immobile.

'Did they predict rain today?' I asked, ever the optimist.

After an embarrassingly long pause, the driver slowly turned and looked at me. 'Are we gonna sit here all night talking about the weather, or do you wanna tell me where ya goin'?'

Must have been a family business as this was obviously the booking bloke's brother, moonlighting as the public relations manager of the town!

'Bowling Club,' I snapped.

There was a deafening squeal of rubber against wet asphalt as he took off and we were hurled against the back seat and, although the trip took less than ten minutes, my whole life rewound in front of me. I had only one thought: we had travelled halfway across Australia in a giant 'truck' in all sorts of conditions, and now our lives were about to end thanks to a kamikaze cabbie in a Commodore!

As this book was not published posthumously, our time wasn't up, but the alcohol we downed to calm our nerves when we finally arrived probably shortened our lives anyway.

The Nelson Bay Bowling Club turned out to be a huge complex with cafeteria-style dining and lots of poker machines. Because we'd been driven by the devil on the trip from Hell, and survived, I decided luck must be with us, and it was worth a dabble on the pokies. And I was right. Waiting outside the club for our taxi ride back to the park, I worked out we had won over one hundred dollars.

We didn't even try and hide our relief when the taxi pulled up with a different driver, but the relief was short-lived. This guy at least smiled, but then took off with an all too familiar squeal of rubber, and as I looked at his reflection in the mirror, I was sure I could detect a family resemblance. His driving style was the same as the first guy, and he managed to complete the ten-minute trip in five. We came to the conclusion there was probably not a lot of excitement in the small township so the boys had to make their own.

18

It was time to do some family bonding with my one and only sibling, so we suggested my Sydney-based brother and sister-in-law meet us in the Hunter Valley for the weekend. They had booked in at one of the many B&Bs in the area, and the understanding host was allowing us to park Winnie in scrubland next to the cottage.

Hon and I arrived in Cessnock, a large town nearby, just after lunch, but were not due at the guest house till six p.m. Cessnock is known as the Mine and Wine Town and, to be honest, we were interested in learning more about one than the other. But knowing my brother's capacity for a 'wee dram', I suspected it was going to be a long and lost weekend, so decided to take a sip of culture first. But then we were guided to the most wonderful automated coal mining exhibit which was housed in the Cessnock Rugby League Supporters Club – and the bar was open. Civilised sightseeing, I'd say!

The afternoon passed easily, and soon it was time to meet up with the rellies. As none of the several hundred maps we had packed highlighted the small township where the guest house was located, we asked for assistance from the gentleman manning reception at the club.

He reached under the counter, produced a small hand-drawn map, and drew a large cross on the right hand side of the page. 'This is where you are at the moment,' he announced.

Did he moonlight at the local information centre? I didn't really care – he was speaking my language.

He then proceeded to fill in the blanks until finally, circling the name of a small town called Pokolbin, looked at us and smiled. 'And Bob's ya uncle!'

'Chris's ya brother' would have been more appropriate, but at least we now knew where we were heading.

I took my duties as navigator very seriously, and was quietly proud of the job I had achieved so far. Well, maybe 'quietly' is a slight exaggeration! We had travelled from South Australia to the northern coast of New South Wales, covering all the places marked on our itinerary, without a hiccup or a slip-up. But this is where it all fell apart!

We had only just left the throbbing metropolis of Cessnock before I wondered if the cartographer responsible for this particular map was dyslexic. Either that or Hon had little faith in my navigational abilities. But surely not!

'We turn left at the second road along here,' I announced.

As we approached the road, the Winnebago swung right.

'No, I said left. You'll have to go back now.'

'I'm fairly sure we should go right,' the Captain responded, and it was a good five minutes before I remembered to close my mouth.

I located my place on the map, and was soon in the navigational swing once more. 'Now there'll be a sign up ahead leading to a vineyard; you take the first road on the right after that.'

Sure enough there was the sign and, as we sailed past, the van took an abrupt turn – to the left.

The look I sent across the driving cabin was pure venom. 'What in hell's teeth are you doing?' I spat through my own clenched ones. 'Don't you know your right from your left?'

Without changing expression, he glanced across at me. 'Don't worry, I've just got a feeling about this area. Pretty sure I know where to go.'

Well, that was all I needed. The map was thrown with great force over my head, and ended up by the bathroom door at the rear of the van.

I wrapped my arms tightly across my heaving chest, as steam escaped from every orifice. 'Fine! Well you just wander around the countryside doing your own thing while I sit here as useless as tits on a bull,' I eloquently stated.

Now I have to say Hon is pretty astute when it comes to recognising the danger signs of a volatile marital situation.

'You're still an excellent Entertainment Officer,' he said, hoping his smile was going to be reciprocated.

Oh yes, there was no doubt in my mind about that. I was certainly entertaining some rather black thoughts about my driver. But as much as it pains me to admit it, we did eventually arrive at the guest house – and on time – and this was achieved by Captain Courageous turning wherever and whenever he cared to, while I maintained the stoniest of silences.

We had only been there ten minutes when we saw the dust of an approaching car. Not only was I thrilled to be catching up with my brother and sister-in-law, I now had a sympathetic audience for my navigation story. But I had forgotten how boys stick together when their driving ability is questioned.

'Don't know what you're worried about, sis,' my brother said. 'You got here, didn't you?'

Perhaps being an only child wouldn't have been so bad!

The guest house was nestled amongst large blue-grey gum trees and native flora, and there were vineyards as far as the eye could see. I did feel a pang of envy as we checked out the quaint cottage accommodation our rellies would be staying in, but was eager to impress upon my brother how well I had adapted to life on the road since those disastrous trips of our childhood. But after offering them a Minnie Winnie Wander and then being unable to even get the door open, all credibility went west.

The proprietor of the guest house had guided us to a clearing a short walk from the cottage and once settled, we were ready for a meal. My wonderfully organised sister-in-law had been researching the local restaurants and made a reservation for dinner at Splash at the Vineyards, an award-winning restaurant specialising in fresh seafood and Hunter beef. The food and wine were superb and the four of us thoroughly enjoyed catching up. More than relatives, these two were our good friends.

We were fairly exhausted by the time we arrived back at the guest house, so said goodnight and walked the short distance to the 'bago. Sitting on the van steps before retiring, I listened to the bush sounds of the night, inhaled the eucalyptus-scented air and breathed a sigh of contentment.

'This is what it's all about.' I smiled at my man, the tension from our earlier trauma forgotten. 'There's nothing like getting back to nature.'

Next day, we decided to visit some local wineries for tasting and purchasing. We made an early start, so by lunchtime the boot of my brother's car was full – and so was I. One of the wineries we visited was Tyrell's, and they just happened to be holding a Red Wine/Red Meat festival with 'over twenty Hunter Valley Wineries featuring their Shiraz'.

Hon and I had passed many a 'happy hour' in the vineyards of the Barossa Valley and McLaren Vale back in South Australia, and felt it was time to compare the New South Wales drop. Naturally we started with a taste of Tyrell's, but then moved on to Saddlers Creek, Ivanhoe, Briar Ridge, McWilliams Mt Pleasant and the Peppertree. Oh yes, and the Audrey Wilkinson turned out to be a saucy little number as well!

The grounds of Tyrell's Wines are lovely, and as we stretched out on the lawn in the warm spring sunshine, sipping wine and listening to the local jazz band, I couldn't think of a better way to spend an afternoon. It was only a cool wind and a dinner reservation that saw us reluctantly leave this beautiful setting.

There is such a wonderful array of restaurants in and around the Hunter Valley and again, my sister-in-law had come up trumps in securing a reservation at another top-class establishment. By this stage, however, the combination of wine and sun was starting to take effect, and my stomach was threatening to rebel at my revelry. Reluctant to ruin dinner plans, I threw myself under the shower, painted on a rather bilious-looking smile, and we were knocking on their cottage door thirty minutes later.

'Let's crack a bottle of champagne,' my brother cheerfully announced.

I was astounded. He had drunk much more than me during the day and was actually suggesting that we keep going.

My stomach relocated itself close to my oesophagus, and I nodded. 'Fine,' I said, and tentatively sipped at a couple of the bubbles.

Suddenly I noticed Hon turn an unusual shade of green.

'You'll have to excuse me – I'm not feeling that good. Think I'll go back to the van and sleep it off,' he said. 'So sorry,' he yelled, as he flew through the door.

Oh no, that was going to be my line! We couldn't both disappear.

I've always been a 'glass half full' kind of girl – and maybe that was the problem – but I was feeling optimistic that things would improve, so followed the others to the car. As soon as we opened the door of the Italian restaurant, a strong aroma of garlic, onions and tomatoes assaulted my nasal passages, and I looked round in desperation.

'Won't be a moment,' I said, a film of sweat appearing on my forehead. 'Catch up with you at the table.' I burst through the door of the toilets, collapsed on the floor and, clutching the refreshingly cold porcelain, begged for my life to end.

But apparently I had not suffered enough! After ten minutes, and a belief I could walk through the restaurant and contain myself plus the afternoon's wine, I felt it was safe to join the others. In my absence, they had ordered a plate of antipasti, 'in case we get hungry waiting for the main course', but as my sister-in-law pushed it across the table I muttered something about saving myself for the main course.

My brother had ordered for me and was confident with his selection. But when the waitress placed a steaming bowl of pasta, covered in rich cream sauce, topped with a mountain of Parmesan cheese, I had to admit defeat.

'Can we change this to take away?' I mumbled, not game to open my mouth too wide.

Glancing at my pathetic pallor, my brother recognised the symptoms – well, he should, he's had six more years' practice – and managed to get the meal and his sister into the car in record time. And thank heavens it was a convertible – the wind in my face was my saving grace!

Back at the guest house, I waved a limp wrist in the direction of my non-dinner companions and staggered up the steps of the van.

SSS (Still Sadly Suffering) slowly raised his leaden head from the pillow. 'Back early?' he said.

'Sick,' I replied.

'Know feeling.'

'Wanna die.'

'Me too.'

'Oooooh,' said in unison.

Even speaking hurts when you're in this condition!

I must have eventually fallen into a coma, but around three a.m. I sat bolt upright, realising the wine still had not fermented sufficiently in my own personal vat. Reluctant to involve Winnie the Poo in this exercise, I burst through the van door, and rushed into the surrounding scrub.

They say everything in nature comes full circle, and as I limply hung on to a branch of a nearby gum tree and called for 'the grapes of Ruth', I returned the produce of the land from whence it came.

As I collapsed on the ground, devoid of the small amount of energy it would have taken to walk the couple of feet to the van, I sensed I was not alone. Assuming my darling and supportive husband had decided to be with his wife in her hour of need, I turned, even mustering a wan smile, but was startled to find a large red kangaroo standing a few feet away. The owners of the guest house had mentioned him on our arrival the previous day, but also issued a warning.

'Don't feed him. Once you start, he can get quite aggressive if the supply isn't constant, and we do feed him pretty well ourselves.'

He was enormous and even larger when he leant back and rested on a tail thicker than my forearm, and drew his long clawed paws into a fairly impressive boxing stance. I decided to remain perfectly still. This was not through any regard for self-preservation, although this would have been the obvious ploy. To tell you the truth, it was an easy decision. I couldn't have even raised an eyebrow, let alone my entire body.

Woman and beast surveyed each other, and you could have heard a cocky's fart. But then something strange happened. It was almost as if this animal had incredible telepathy, and knew I was already a beaten spirit.

He slowly lowered his front paws to the ground, and gazed at me for a few more seconds. 'Tsk, tsk, tsk,' he clicked, and I felt suitably chastised.

Who said animals were dumb?

19

The next morning we felt much better – it would have been physically impossible to feel worse – and although our dinner the previous evening had been a disaster, it was still a good catch-up with relatives we don't see enough of. But now it was time for each couple to head off in different directions.

Even though we had been travelling away from the coast the minute we left Nelson Bay, it hadn't really impacted on me as yet. But when the lush green vineyards of the Hunter Valley were replaced by the reds and ochres of the interior, I knew we were heading 'out back' again, and it was no surprise to find the name Dubbo meant 'red earth'.

Although we found at least eight caravan parks listed in Dubbo, the choice was made fairly simple by one small fact. The one we chose was right next door to the bowling club. We opted for an early meal, as our evening had already been planned.

'How about checking this out,' said Hon, reaching across the breakfast table and handing me a brochure on the Dubbo Conservatory. 'Discover a hugely magnified moon, the Planets, the Milky Way and beyond, with the most Hi-Tech telescopes in the West.'

Not having a penchant for things in the cosmos, I was finding enough to fascinate me on our own planet, but realised this was something LSD (Long-suffering Darling) really wanted to do. After all, he had waited patiently outside numerous shops across the countryside while I indulged in some retail therapy. I owed him.

In order to reach the Conservatory, we had to travel along a dark road in countryside that was so bare it resembled the moon's surface. After fifteen minutes of depressingly barren scenery, I was ready to suggest we call this our galactic experience and head back to the caravan park. The brochure stated the show would commence at seven thirty. I was intrigued – were the planets having their make-up done and donning sparkling costumes ready for the curtain to rise at the designated time?

Pulling into a dirt car park, we entered the small corrugated iron shed and were surprised to see half a dozen groups of people standing around waiting for some sort of direction. A man, sporting a grizzled beard and very little dress sense, stood behind a makeshift counter talking loudly to a young Japanese couple. Judging from their puzzled expressions, however, the increased volume was not assisting their language comprehension.

It was seven-thirty-nine before we were ushered through a door behind the counter, and I assumed Mars was having difficulty locating her outfit.

Our friend from the counter waited while we seated ourselves on wooden benches and then dramatically cleared his throat. 'Hello, everyone, my name is Arthur. Welcome to the hobby that grew.'

Polite laughter greeted this statement, and Arthur seemed pleased with his receptive audience. As he began talking, it was obvious he had a love of all things astral. It wasn't the content of the speech which had me fascinated, however, but the uncomfortably breathy voice it was delivered in. Each time he inhaled it sounded like the last gasps of a dying man. Certainly not the most relaxed speaker, and I wondered whether this wheeze was the result of too many cold nights spent stargazing. After one final gasp, he smiled and announced he was ready for some audience participation. Questions were fired at the group and, noting his penetrating gaze, I wondered if he had been a schoolteacher in a previous life.

'How many light years would it take to travel to the outer edge of our solar system?' he asked, pointing his finger directly at me.

My knowledge of astronomy was limited to a few planet names and Neil Armstrong's 'one giant leap' back in 1969. Perhaps if I just kept quiet I would blend into the surroundings.

'Well – what do you think? Yes, you,' he stressed, just so there was no misunderstanding.

Unfortunately his finger was still pointing directly at me, and I realised my blending ability needed serious work.

'Six trillion, three billion, forty-seven million light years,' I said, adding a smile in case he thought I was serious.

'Nup, you're way off,' he said, throwing me a look of disdain.

Bugger! Perhaps I should have made it only four trillion. Why didn't he ask Galileo sitting next to me? It was his bright idea to come in the first place, and he loved brainteasers.

After another fifteen minutes of information, my head was bursting with mathematical equations. At this point, Arthur decided to give up on finding any intelligent life form in the shed and announced there would be two short films, providing us with information about our fascinating solar system. The wooden benches were starting to make a deep impression through my jeans, and the cold wind outside had found a gap in the corrugated iron. I glanced at Hon but he was already in another world.

But surprisingly, the amateur videos more than held my interest. Arthur's plan was working as I felt a frisson of excitement about 'stuff in the sky'. Ten minutes later the screen faded to black, and Arthur emerged from the gloom. We were invited to follow him outside so we could see the real thing and, as the group shuffled forward, we were guided to a coat rack containing several tired parkas.

'Can get pretty chilly out there, folks, so help yourselves,' Arthur gasped.

Assuming this would not be a fashion statement I cared to remember, I was quite happy to grab the nearest parka. My arms and hands immediately disappeared in amongst the fleecy depths, and the hem of the parka brushed my shinbone. At least now I would only be bored, but not cold. Outside, there was a raised cement platform holding two enormous telescopes.

Arthur darted over to one and started to make adjustments. 'Now, ladies and gentlemen, I was going to start by showing you Alpha Centauri and Beta Centauri, but it appears they're hiding behind some clouds.'

What a pity! Oh well, perhaps we could go home now?

But in the next laboured breath, Arthur announced that if we waited two minutes, the cloud would pass and the planets would be visible. I wondered if our astronomer dabbled in astrology also, as exactly two minutes later (and believe me, I was counting) he was dancing round the telescope.

'Here we go. Line up, everyone. You can see them clearly now,' he announced.

I watched fascinated, as the group separated into two distinct categories. One group, the 'I wanna be first' people, pushed and shoved to secure a front position. The second group were politeness personified. 'No, you go first, please' and 'Here, hop in front of me. I can wait.'

I fitted into a third category and was probably the sole member. The 'now that my face is frozen solid, I shall kill anyone who takes a long look' group.

When my turn finally arrived, I mounted the platform and tried to peer through the eyehole. This presented immediate difficulties, as my eye and the telescope had no hope of meeting, even in the distant future.

Arthur, sensing my dilemma, walked over and assessed the situation. 'I'll have to adjust this telescope for you – it's meant for taller people.'

Was it my imagination or was his voice overly loud? Not only was everyone aware of my lack of knowledge when it came to astronomy, but now I had created difficulties through being vertically challenged. But soon the appropriate adjustments had been made, and I squinted through the lens.

Well, there was certainly a 'wow' factor here! I felt as if I had travelled all those light years and was about to touchdown into a strange world. I even started to experience some of the excitement Arthur had been displaying earlier.

'That's absolutely amazing!' I cried.

Arthur's expression spoke volumes: now it dawns on her!

We filled in the next hour with telescopes being pointed in different directions, and Arthur extolling the wonders of the heavens. This kept me occupied for a while, but I soon became aware of a chill around my ankles. Glancing at my watch, I was relieved to see this adventure was nearly at an end. But just as Arthur was wrapping up his presentation, a familiar voice carried across the night air.

'How long is light visible in space, and could this be increased with greater magnification?'

Arthur turned to look at Galileo, and beamed. Now he had a legitimate excuse to carry on for another half an hour. It was at this point I knew, without a shadow of doubt, that given the right circumstances, I was actually capable of murdering my husband!

Arthur moved over, and standing next to his star pupil, proceeded to drag up even more mathematical equations – at least I think that's what he was doing. I was too fascinated watching the tribal dance taking place between teacher and student.

As Arthur leant forward to stress a point, Hon would take a step backwards. Arthur would then step forward once again and my man would take another backwards step.

After what seemed like several light years, Arthur decided the question had been sufficiently answered, and we were allowed to return to the warm shed. Everyone thanked Arthur profusely and as we made our way to the door, I paused to pat the rather lean cat sitting on the counter.

'That's Alpha,' Arthur explained. 'His mate Beta's at home tonight. Beta hates the cold.'

Now that's my kind of cat!

As we walked across the car park, I turned to Galileo and frowned. 'Why on earth would you ask a question when you could see he was winding down?' I asked. 'And what was with the fancy footwork?'

He looked sheepish. 'Believe me, I regretted the question as soon as he walked over. I know why he doesn't feel the cold though – his old mate, Johnny Walker. His breath nearly knocked me out!'

We still talk of Arthur to this day, and I smile when I recall that heavenly night. It's not that I've suddenly developed an interest in the night sky, or even felt the need to rush out and buy a telescope. No, it's the honorary title we bestowed upon our new friend as we drove back to the caravan park – Arthur the Asthmatic Alcoholic Astronomer.

20

Thanks to our new friend Arthur, I was now much more knowledgeable about things 'up there'. So as we packed up the next morning to leave Dubbo, it was my suggestion to stop off at Parkes to see the large radio telescope housed there. The literature was quite informative:

> This is a 64-metre dish which astronomers use to study the heavens and examine a wide range of radio energies from our galaxy and other parts of the universe. It is not only responsible for the television pictures of the first moonwalks, but the rescue of Apollo 13 and, in more recent years, has collected data from spacecraft at Uranus, Halley's Comet, Neptune and Jupiter.

Okay, that's the 'Arthur' part taken care of! I was more fascinated with the fact that it had been the star of a great Australian movie *The Dish*. Made by the talented Working Dog team, this film is a comedy based on Australia's role in the Apollo 11 mission in July 1969. It wasn't surprising to hear that visitor numbers to the observatory almost doubled after the release of this movie.

But even before you go inside and wander around the displays, there are a number of interesting exhibits outside. Two 'whispering dishes', set a hundred metres apart, are extremely popular with visitors. If two people position themselves at the centre of each dish, they can communicate quite easily merely by whispering. This, dear reader, demonstrates the focusing power of a paraboloid – the Parkes dish being one. Stick that in your spacecraft, Arthur!

While we were both fascinated by the paraboloid phenomena, I'm still wondering why I needed to take a photo of Hon standing in front of one of these dishes. They say a picture may be worth a thousand words, but this particular one wasn't talking (or even whispering) and didn't even make the photo album!

What's the speed of light? Three hundred thousand kilometres per hour. What is the Milky Way? A galaxy one hundred and twenty thousand light years across. What does a quasar do? Radiates the power of a thousand galaxies.

I do realise a little knowledge is not only a dangerous thing, but can also be pretty boring, but where the hell are you now, Arthur, when I know all the answers?

About five minutes out of Parkes, I started thinking about lunch. As if I didn't have enough to do, I had not only taken on the task of Navigator and Entertainment Officer, but also unselfishly offered my services as organiser of the 'Food and Sustenance Team' – FAST – which is how we liked our food!

Thirty-three kilometres later, we were driving into the rural settlement of Forbes on the Lachlan River, and this seemed as good a place as any to fill up our tanks. This town is full of history and has some magnificent buildings. The post office, imposingly situated on a corner block is the original building – a very grand place for the one postal officer who used to cope with a population of fifteen thousand back in the 1860s!

The Albion Hotel occupies another corner block and was completed in the early 1890s. It not only sold the greatest quantity of alcohol in Australia during the 1860s, but was also the stopover point for the Cobb and Co. coaches. There's a pretty impressive tower on top that was used as a lookout for approaching coaches, and a tunnel underneath where the gold was sent through to be loaded on to the coaches. And gold was the reason this town became famous – or perhaps that should be infamous.

When gold was discovered in 1861, many people were drawn to the district, not least the bushrangers, who wanted their riches the easy way. Ben Hall was only twelve years old when he came to the district, and at the age of twenty-three he purchased a station. He was tried and acquitted for armed robbery in 1862, but when he came back to the property his house had been burnt down, his cattle were dead and his wife had run off with a former policeman.

It was at this point that he decided to become a full-time bushranger, the brochure stated. As opposed to what? A casual bushranger with unpaid public holidays?

He and his gang pulled off the largest Australian gold robbery of the century in 1862 and he was shot and killed twenty kilometres north-west of Forbes. And even his death was dramatic, according to the article in the daily newspaper.

> It took one police inspector, a sergeant, five troopers and two black trackers to hunt Ben Hall down. Two shots were initially fired, both hitting their mark, but failing to stop him. Then the five troopers took over and finally Mr Hall appeared injured. He supported himself on a gum sapling and called out, 'I am wounded. Shoot me dead.'

Not only did they find thirty bullets in his body, but he was also carrying 'three loaded revolvers, 70 pounds in cash, three gold chains and the miniature of a female'. Miniature of a female what?

He is buried at the Forbes Cemetery, along with Ned Kelly's sister, Kate, who drowned in the Lachlan River in 1898, and Captain Cook's great-grand-niece Rebecca Shields. Yes, I thought the last one was drawing a fairly long bow as an important grave site, but I guess we wouldn't be here if it wasn't for the Captain.

I have to admit I do like a bad boy, and so does the township of Forbes. There's a large statue of Ben Hall outside the Lachlan Vintage Village, and even the local motor inn carries his name. I'm sure he was just stealing all that gold so he could share it with the poor people of the district – and Paris Hilton's a natural blonde! Yes, well worth a stop.

In preparing for this road trek, we were determined to maintain a balance of driving and recreational hours, and I saw the immediate need for yet another list.

But Hon disagreed. 'Now this is the sort of thing your spreadsheet is ideal for,' said my own personal accountant.

I have managed to work for a number of years in the financial services sector and avoided using anything but the simplest spreadsheet – and that's just fine with me. Give me words over figures any day. I commented to my brother once about Hon's 'fetish with financials' that always led to a spate of spreadsheets, but silly me – my brother's an accountant as well.

'You don't realise how easy they make life,' he said. 'I've set up spreadsheets for everything in my life.'

Whoopee! Yes, all right. It was easier to work out the distances, but if Hon ever brings this up, I'll deny admitting it.

After agreeing on our night at Dubbo, my suggestion of Albury–Wodonga as the next stopover was not met with resounding enthusiasm.

'You realise that'll be over five hundred and sixty kilometres we'll be travelling in one day?' Hon said.

I told you I wasn't good with numbers. I peered at the small figures on the map. 'How about Wagga Wagga then?'

The spreadsheet was fed some more numbers, but Hon frowned. 'That's still over four hundred kilometres. No, let's make it West Wyalong.'

I could see how this was panning out – WWI versus WWII – war had been declared. I must have had an inkling, even at that early stage, that Hon would be responsible for most of the driving responsibility, so I graciously gave in.

By the time we drove into West Wyalong, it was early evening, and when we found a centrally located caravan park, we checked in. It really didn't matter which town we were in that night, as it had been a fairly exhausting day. So exhausting, I couldn't even be bothered going out for a meal. So exhausting, I couldn't even be bothered cooking a meal in the van. We had paté and biscuits for dinner!

Let me formally apologise to the people of WWII and say that I'm sure West Wyalong has a wonderful history and many things for the tourist to see – but unfortunately we didn't. Even though caravan parks are not the quietest of accommodation venues, we both managed to sleep until nine-fifty-five the next morning. Our next overnight was Albury/Wodonga, a little over three hundred kilometres away, so we were loath to linger.

But as we drove up the main street, I was able to relate one piece of information about West Wyalong to take away with us. 'Dymphna Cusack was born here in 1902,' I announced. 'You know, the bird who wrote *Come In Spinner* with Florence James.'

Hon looked suitably unimpressed, but I was merely musing. I associate her more with the book *Caddie*, the story of a Sydney barmaid in the 1920s and 1930s. The author was known only as 'Caddie', and this was a nickname given to her because, as one man put it, 'She had class – like a Cadillac.' She took a job as housekeeper at a cottage in the Blue Mountains, where Dymphna and Florence were writing *Come In Spinner*. Caddie was drawn to this position, as she knew the two women were writers and she had always thought her own life would make an interesting story. Both Dymphna and Florence agreed and encouraged her to write it down, and there is a foreword in the book by Cusack. There was a great film made starring Helen Morse and Jackie Weaver, which I've seen several times over the years.

I hadn't been optimistic about finding fodder for my Fascinating Facts folder in this town. For a start, we hadn't spent much time in the area, and it seemed that no sooner had we completed our arrival checklist, than we were getting ready to depart. But now we could leave WWII, confident the battle had been won!

I can understand why a town is named West Wyalong – it wants to separate itself from East Wyalong. But I couldn't seem to find the eastern section of Wyalong on any map. And why do they put Albury–Wodonga together? If the forefathers of the region had wanted one township, surely it would have been a simple enough decision to settle on either one side of the Murray River, or the other. These towns straddle the Murray and no matter which side you reside on, you live in Albury–Wodonga. Perhaps it was time for a new name. I liked the sound of Alburdonga – it definitely had an Aboriginal feel to it – and I could already hear myself explaining its origins: 'The literal translation, from the Wiradjuri language of course, is "two towns kept apart by the silver serpent of dreamtime".'

Sixteen kilometres out of Albury–Wodonga is the Ettamogah Pub. This was the inspiration of the cartoonist Ken Maynard, who lived in Albury (no mention of Wodonga in his history) and wrote a comic strip in which he depicted the goings-on at an imaginary hotel. We were told it was an Aboriginal word meaning 'place of good drink'. Wonder what 'billabong' means? The pub was built in 1987 and is an exact replica of the cartoon pub, complete with the impossible design of outward leaning walls and verandas, a truck on the roof and a tree that stands right in the middle of the place and reaches through the upper level.

These days the Ettamogah Pub is the centrepiece of a tourist village that is brimming with attractions and activities. The complex houses a pottery shop and a blacksmith's shop and the lock-up, in case 'anyone decides to come the raw prawn'. And talking of signs, they're not short of them here.

'A ten-ounce glass of beer is about as handy as the bottom half of a mermaid.' This had to be some male's brainchild. I'd say any passing mermaids could take issue with that.

'Beware of the Agapanthus – do not run.' This insinuates that agapanthus do something. Mine only hang their heads just before they die.

'For sale – 110 ferrets, 4 nets, 1 useless cattle dog, 3 prisoners and 2 cats.' I put in an offer for the ferrets, dog and cats but they weren't interested in separating this lot.

We sometimes cringe at any over-the-top display of kitsch Australiana, but if I had friends visiting from overseas, this would be just the sort of thing I would take them to see.

We would love to have spent a bit longer at this wonderful pub, but we were heading towards Gundagai, and had to check out the famous statue of that dog on that box. The stories told round this piece of Australian folklore are fascinating, and depending which version you believe, the dog can be painted as a villain or a hero.

They were tough times when men had to transport supplies along makeshift tracks over rough terrain by bullock teams. Often they were bogged or had to wait for the river level to fall, and would fill in time by reciting rhymes. And if the men needed to leave camp and seek help, it was the dog's job to guard its master's tuckerbox and possessions. I could understand the men being moved to verse by the dog's loyalty.

And then there's version two with corrected spelling! The dog 'shat' on its master's tuckerbox and ruined everything inside. When it ate a bait and died, the master laid it to rest in the very same tuckerbox!

There is not only confusion over the part the dog played in all this, but exactly how far out of Gundagai this happened, if in fact it did at all! Some say it was at Snake Gully, five miles out of the township, where the famous monument now stands as a tribute to the pioneers of Australia, and symbolises the mateship between man and dog. But others swear the real event occurred nine miles out of Gundagai, as mentioned in the famous poem by Jack Moses.

But either way, I don't think it matters, least of all to the dogs of Australia. Isn't their whole world a toilet?

21

'Should that be flashing?' I asked, leaning over and pointing to a small light on the dashboard.

We had just reached the outskirts of Canberra, and were looking forward to finding a caravan park where we could settle for the night.

Hon glanced down and frowned. 'No, I don't think so,' he said. 'Wonder what it means?'

His calm disposition had been the saving grace in many situations, but I didn't feel it appropriate at this point.

'I think we should pull over,' I said, reluctant to take my eyes off the light for a minute.

'It can't be anything too serious,' he said, giving a casual shrug, 'It's only just started flashing.'

How did he know? Had he been watching it all the time just in case it blinked? If so, what was he doing taking his eyes off the road?

'Look, I'm not panicking,' I said, panicking, 'but I think we should switch the engine off, just in case.'

'And what would that achieve? We'd be better off finding a dealership and letting the mechanic take a look.'

Ten minutes later we stood behind the cleanest car mechanic I had encountered and waited for the verdict.

'Can't say what the problem is at the moment. It won't be anything serious. These are pretty reliable vehicles, and they would have given it a full check before renting. Can you leave her with us? I can take a better look in the morning.'

It was five-thirty, and as we had caught them just before they closed for the day, we nodded.

'Oh, hang on,' the mechanic said, 'I just remembered. We've got a really big job booked in tomorrow – it'll probably take all day. We may not get round to looking at yours till the next day,' he said. 'Is that going to throw your plans out too much?'

What alternative did we have? As a mechanic, Hon was a pretty impressive accountant, and I had opted for commercial college over trade school. Besides, from the number of brochures we had on Canberra, two months wouldn't have been long enough to cover all the tourist attractions.

'You're going to need some wheels for a couple of days,' he said, dragging a set of keys from his pocket, and tossing them in our direction. He pointed to the other side of the yard. 'Take the Corolla over there – nothing flash, but at least you'll be able to get around.'

We threw an assortment of clothes into two small bags, locked Winnie, and headed to our surrogate transport. The mechanic was right. There was nothing flash about the car, but at least the engine turned over and the lights on the dashboard didn't – flash, that is.

Realising we were leaving our accommodation behind as well, I had grabbed the directory which not only supplied details of every caravan park in Australia, but motels as well. The choice was mind-blowing, so we concentrated on the medium price range. But that wasn't our most difficult task. We then had to decipher the secret code attached to each listing.

RO (room only), BLB (bed and light breakfast), CABLE (Hon's eyes lit up), BLKTS (blankets); as opposed to what – hessian bags? JCC (Japanese Credit Cards) – would we get a better room if we had one? PEN CON (the old pensioner concession). Only a few years to wait! And we soon learnt there was no rule to say we must stay at a motel just because we had made an enquiry of availability at reception.

'Why don't you go and have a look around and see what else is on offer – everyone else does,' the first motel owner suggested. He was either very confident of the facilities his establishment offered or just couldn't be bothered with a short-term booking.

We decided to take him up on his offer, and were soon checking out numbers two to four on our hastily made list. But I did feel a little awkward turning down accommodation, as the owners proudly showed us their rooms and waited for an enthusiastic response.

'It's lovely,' I heard myself say to motel owner number two, 'but this is only our first stop. We'll just pop in to a couple of others, but I'm sure we'll be back.'

That sounded so pathetic, I was determined to come up with a better excuse at the next motel.

'What a lovely room! It looks very comfortable, and you have such nice coloured towels in the bathroom' (admittedly I was struggling for positives) 'but I've just realised you don't provide a barbecue. You see, we won the meat raffle at the bowling club last night and wanted to cook it up for dinner. Thanks, anyway.' I was heading for the door as I spoke. After all, mine host might have a small tripod barbecue tucked away at the back of the motel by the industrial waste bins he wanted to share with us.

I had mentally crossed the third motel from our list even before we pulled into the driveway, but Hon was determined to check out all options. The owner, a woman in her late sixties, would not have been out of place in an English seaside boarding house; the sort that accommodated small repertory groups which toured the country back in the 1950s.

She was an angular woman with dangerously sharp features and darting bird-like eyes. The only relief on a face coated with layers of pancake make-up was an orange slash painted on lips so thin they threatened to disappear inside her mouth. As she opened the door to unit eleven, she threw her head back and yawned loudly. 'Sorry about that – bit tired – I was out dancing last night – and the night before – and three times last week. I tell you, it's been all go since Harry died.'

Another tonsil stretcher followed this statement, and I immediately lost interest in the DB (double bed) and AC (air conditioning).

'I'm so sorry – was Harry your husband?'

'Yes, for more years than I care to remember.' She suddenly realised how this sounded. 'Oh, don't get me wrong. He was a good man in his own way, just boring, poor love.' Her thin pencilled eyebrows shot towards the ceiling. 'His idea of a fun night was two glasses of sherry instead of the usual one.'

The three of us paused for a few seconds in memory of Harry.

Suddenly our merry widow smiled. 'What a pity you weren't in town last night. You could've come to the exhibition. Oh, it was lovely. Everyone dresses to the nines, and the music and the frocks – it was wonderful!' She screwed up one eye, and I recognised a wink. 'Shouldn't say it, I know, but I did look pretty good.'

'Ballroom dancing – how exciting,' I said, smiling my encouragement for her to continue.

Leaning towards me, she dropped her voice. 'I don't tell everyone this, love, but I shop out of town for my frocks. That way there's no wardrobe dysfunction.' She seemed pleased with her turn of phrase. 'Someone else with the same frock,' she added, just in case we were slow on the uptake.

I could imagine how this would be a disaster in the world of mirror balls and tulle. 'Do you have the same partner each night?' I asked, easing myself onto the edge of the bed.

'Well, there is one gentleman,' she said, a slight blush managing to fight its way through the pancake, 'and has he got some moves, that one.'

I desperately hoped we were still talking about ballroom dancing.

Suddenly my own dance partner cleared his throat. 'Yes, well, this is only the first place we've seen, so we'll probably check out a few others.'

Damn it! I had so many other questions. Sure, the accommodation wasn't anything to write home about, but this woman's story was. I reluctantly followed Hon to the car.

'I get the feeling there's a lot more to her life story – I'd love to have heard it,' I said, wishing Hon's curiosity about people matched mine.

'I tell you what – why don't I go for a round of golf tomorrow, and you can take her out for lunch. That way we're both happy!' Hon said, grinning.

We had just pulled into the car park of the fourth motel so I swallowed the smart retort as I realised that this time, we had struck gold. It was a two-storey colonial building with private balconies leading from each unit and a profusion of potted colour everywhere.

'I don't care what the inside looks like, we're staying here,' I stated. If someone was going to put this much effort into the outside presentation, I was fairly confident this attention to detail would be continued throughout the entire complex.

As we stepped into the reception area, a small wraith-like vision crept from behind a beaded curtain.

'Yeeeees?' the woman whispered.

Long dark hair liberally peppered with silver streaks had been lazily caught up in a bun on top of her head, and a long dark knitted jacket swept the ground around her feet. Her small white hands were clutched tightly to her chest, and even though I have yet to reach five foot on the doctor's wall chart, I had to look down to make eye contact. I was rather surprised this nervous little woman had chosen an occupation which necessitated dealing with the general public. She looked terrified of her own shadow, let alone anyone else's.

'We'd like a room for two nights, thanks,' I said, stepping forward.

She crept over to a large book on the counter and slowly opened it. 'Yes – two nights, you say – let me see – well – I'm not really sure.'

Now within moments of staring at the book, I had ascertained there were five rooms in the complex with scattered bookings over the next two nights.

'Mmm – I've got Mr and Mrs Baker in this one tonight,' she continued, the brow furrowed in deep concentration, 'but it is free tomorrow night. No, wait a minute, that won't do. Oh, here we are – these people are coming in tomorrow so you could have their room tonight. Oh, wait a minute, that means we'd have to move you for tomorrow night.'

I had to use every bit of self-control not to leap over the desk, grab an eraser, and re-organise the guest list. 'For heaven's sake, woman,' I mentally yelled, 'put Mr and Mrs Baker in room number three and that frees up number two for both nights.'

I will admit I have a decidedly short wick in some situations, but even Hip (He of Infinite Patience) was starting to fidget.

Suddenly our nervous chatelaine looked up and a frisson of relief passed across her face. 'Look, I think I can put the Bakers in number three, and then you could have number two – yes, that would work.'

I almost cheered as she grabbed a key from the board behind her.

'Walk this way,' she whispered.

How? Like a member of the Addam's family?

Suddenly she stopped, turned round, and frowned. 'By the way, I don't allow smoking in my rooms,' she added.

I thought for a minute the woman was psychic, until I realised we had just finished our cigarettes before we pulled into the car park, and the smell must have lingered on our clothes.

'Please don't worry about that. We do smoke but never inside, and we have our own ashtrays.' If I was expecting brownie points for this statement, I was to be disappointed.

'My daughter helps out here,' she continued, as if I hadn't even spoken, 'and she has slight asthma. If you smoke in the room, she'll be able to tell me. She could be off for days gasping for breath,' she murmured through pursed lips.

I reassured her once again, but she didn't seem convinced.

By this time we had arrived at apartment two, and I was surprised to see not one, but two large mats by the front door. And complementing this carpet of coir was a rather frightening-looking boot scraper in the shape of a duck with a demented dial. In case the message was still not clear, a large sign dominated the door of the apartment: 'Please, please wipe your shoes before you come inside.'

I must have resembled a dog trying to locate a suitable toilet spot as I scuffed my feet on both mats and gave the duck's back a rather vigorous massage.

She glanced nervously at our shoes. 'Yes, I suppose you two will be all right, but some people go for walks in sneakers – they pick up all sorts of things,' she stated ominously.

What a novel idea! Not only can you get fit when you walk, but also use it a sample collecting exercise. Time and motion at its best! I might even get myself a larger pair of runners. Now our shoes were close to pristine, we were invited to step inside the apartment, and were not surprised to find the beautifully maintained façade had been continued inside.

'This is delightful,' I said, but the glance she sent in my direction was obviously meant to curb my enthusiasm.

'You can fix a simple breakfast if you like, but we don't allow cooking in the rooms. We can't get rid of the smell.'

When we stood in the Winnebago a few hours ago contemplating what we should pack for a couple of nights, I did toy with the idea of dismantling the stove and bringing it with us. Just as well I hadn't bothered!

'Some Asian guests bring briefcases with them,' she continued, in a hoarse whisper, 'and inside they have a stove and a gas bottle.'

Horror was radiating from her eyes like small darts. She waited for a reaction, but I could only think of one thing. If you can fit a stove, plus a gas cylinder into a case, I'd hardly call it brief! I wandered over to the bed and sat down.

'The bed's nice and comfortable. I'm sure we'll have a good rest.'

I paused as a sign next to the bed caught my eye: 'Dear Valued Guest, please do not use oils near donna covers.'

I wondered who this Donna Covers was; maybe the daughter with the overactive olfactory organ.

But our lady of the manor hadn't quite completed her instruction manual. 'Don't leave the heating on all the time. My husband comes and switches it on for you,' she said.

That should be interesting. Particularly if we're in the throes of passion tonight and there's a knock on the door followed by a male voice asking, 'Is it hot enough in there?'

'I don't like to think of this place as a motel,' she said, a welcome interruption to the vision forming in my mind. 'We don't leave folded towels on the end of the bed.' Her look intimated this was considered rather bourgeois.

We had moved into the bathroom by this stage, and I noticed several folded towels on the vanity bar. Yes, I could see the difference that made! I was sorely tempted to suggest she call it a boarding house; I was certainly bored with all the instructions.

You'll probably be surprised to hear we finally decided to take her up on her warm invitation, but we were so exhausted by this stage, and I was getting excited about sharing a large bed with my man once again.

Fortunately we only glimpsed 'She Who Must Be Obeyed' in the distance over the next two days; that was mainly because we ran like the wind if we saw her coming.

When we did check out two days later, there was a new sign on the outside wall of the units that read 'Gentlemen must not clean their windscreens and then wash their rags in the sink.' Where would she suggest washing them– the toilet?

This was just one too many signs. I ran back inside and glanced around at the many signs adorning the room. And then the one on the dining room table caught my eye: 'Please do not move table – it marks the carpet.'

I picked up the edge of the table and rearranged each leg two centimetres from their original indentations. Yes, childish, I admit. But even more so was my desire to hide in the wardrobe and wait for her to make this horrific discovery!

22

Like most Australians, I feel a sense of pride on Anzac Day when I watch the grizzled faces of our last remaining diggers, and the rapidly ageing faces of our Vietnam veterans, as they march through the city streets. But I have to admit I rarely give these heroes a second thought. So I was only mildly curious about the War Memorial in Canberra.

We arrived just in time to join a guided tour, and the first thing I noticed about our guide was the small service pin on his left lapel. Although he had a crisp head of steel grey hair standing to attention, and a neat toothbrush moustache to match, the face was not old enough to have been part of either Big War. He had to be closer to my own age, so was probably a Vietnam vet. But not one of the unlucky marbles of conscription! No, this man had career army stamped all over him.

Within five minutes of the tour beginning, he started firing questions at the motley group of tourists gathered around him, and the pauses were more than pregnant as we searched our brains for answers, and he waited with ill-concealed impatience.

'Where's the Tomb of the Unknown Soldier?' he barked.

The only sound was the shuffle of feet.

'Westminster Abbey.' Did I say that out loud? No, thank God – it might be wrong, and this early in the tour I was reluctant to show my complete naivety regarding war history.

He didn't even try to conceal his disappointment. 'It's Westminster Abbey,' he announced, his voice carrying across the quadrangle.

Bugger! Oh well, I'll be ready for the next question.

We moved to a long section of wall containing the names of men and women who died serving their country. Red poppies were dotted along the wall, left there by relatives and friends who had identified their loved ones. Maybe this whole experience would mean more to me if I had lost someone.

Twenty-five minutes later we were still standing at the wall, and the information was starting to wash over me like a cold shower. I turned and glanced at Hon, and not even needing words, knew he was feeling the same. We quietly slipped away from the tour, secretly dreading the command to stay with the crowd, but our guide was too busy.

'Why was Simpson famous?' we heard our military friend ask the group. 'And don't tell me it was because he carried injured soldiers on his donkey.'

'There goes my answer!' I thought. Our departure was well timed.

Now we were able to wander around by ourselves, I experienced a stirring of interest. My father had joined the Royal Australian Air Force at the beginning of World War II, but spoke little of his war service. He had never marched on Anzac Day, feeling that because his time was spent in Australia, he did not deserve to be recognised with those who had gone overseas.

'Wasn't he contributing to the war effort just as much?' I asked Mum one day.

She agreed, but with Dad it was a closed subject.

I looked up and noticed I was standing in front of the re-creation of a prison barracks, where the Japanese housed our captured soldiers. How did any of them survive? My heart clenched as I looked at photos of these smiling but emaciated men, standing with their arms casually flung round each other's shoulders, recognising that the camaraderie was a vital part of their survival. I turned to see where Hon was and noticed his deep concentration as he stood reading the story about one of the photographs.

I wandered through an archway and entered a small alcove devoted to the women who served in this war. One of the most emotional pictures painted of any war is the reality of mothers waving goodbye to their sons, never knowing whether they would see them again. But other family members were just as involved. Parents kissing their daughters goodbye, sisters farewelling their sisters.

These young women were heading overseas, dressed in khaki and white veils, and some only looked in their late teens. When I was that age, my biggest challenge was finding the right outfit to wear to the dance club on Saturday night.

My boys' paternal grandmother was a nursing sister in World War II and sometimes spoke of her time in Borneo repatriating prisoners from Changi Prison, before they were sent home. 'We couldn't let the families see the damage the incarceration had done to these men's minds and bodies,' she said, the painful memory flashing across her face. She had witnessed man's cruelty to man first hand, and her lack of enthusiasm when I told her I was visiting Japan in 1971 became understandable.

But not all her memories were sad. 'On one of our days off, the heat was so stifling, some of the soldiers asked us to join them down the beach for a swim,' she said smiling. 'Well, let's say the army didn't feel swimsuits a necessary part of our regulation kit, so we stole tea towels from the mess hut and made two-piece bathers from them.'

The lines round her eyes formed even deeper creases at the memory, and I could see her as a young girl, a long tangle of dark brown curls brushing her shoulders, swept back from her face with tortoiseshell clips and her young, slim body running towards the waves. Even into her late seventies, she still kept in contact with her fellow nurses, and although she had a wide circle of friends, these girls had a very special bond.

By this stage, Hon had caught up and we moved through to a large auditorium. Several aircraft from that period were eerily suspended from the ceiling and a screen wrapped around three-quarters of the room announcing an interactive display would begin in five minutes. We climbed to the viewing platform and waited quietly with the small crowd. Suddenly the lights dimmed, and the screen sprung to life. We were at a small English airfield watching pilots preparing for a night raid over Berlin in the famous Lancaster G bombers. Inside the barracks young women sat at radios, monitoring the start of the operation.

'They were lovely lads, the Australians,' a lilting Irish colleen announced, 'so much fun, and quite handsome as well. We became such close friends.'

The pilots climbed into their cockpits, and with one final order, took off across the English Channel. Static radio contact was maintained between aircraft, those wonderful Aussie accents betraying little fear. Although the flight time was reduced for us, you still had a sense of suppressed tension from the crew, during what must have seemed an endless flight. Then a harsher voice cut across the radio with the order to release their bombs.

We were over Berlin; the night sky turned to daylight, the noise and confusion overpowering. The camera travelled down to the streets of Berlin, and there was a different sort of noise and confusion, but still as intense, as terrified families ran towards air raid shelters, and harsh guttural commands cut across the high-pitched sirens. Mothers scooped small children into their arms, terror written on their faces, as explosions erupted around them. And then we were back in the cockpit of the Lancaster and the order was clear – head for home.

The journey back to England was interspersed with more static radio messages, but the atmosphere was sombre. The harsh squeal of tyres touching the tarmac jolted us from our shock, and we watched the pilots climb down from their cockpits, strain etched on their young faces. Back in the radio operator's room, the women's faces were grim. Numbers on a blackboard now carried a harsh chalk line through the middle, and our Irish girl's voice echoed round the auditorium once again.

'We lost fifty planes that night and twice as many crew – those beautiful Australians we laughed with only yesterday – we will miss them.' Her voice broke.

Slowly the lights of the auditorium came on, and my face was wet with tears. I wanted to sob out loud, but was frightened that once I started, I might not stop. There was a tight fist grabbing my heart, and I was having difficulty forming words. I couldn't believe I'd nearly missed this! Maybe if I had gone with high expectations I might have been disappointed – but I don't think so. There are times in your life when you experience something so profound you know the memory will stay with you for a very long time. And the next morning when I woke up, the emotions of the young pilots and the look of terror on the German civilians' faces were the first things I thought of.

We stayed in Canberra for three days. Not because there was anything seriously wrong with the Winnebago – just the opposite, in fact. About the only thing our mechanic friend could find was a globe that needed replacing. There was a lovely touch to our 'dealership dealings' as well. Six months after we arrived home, we received a letter from them saying they'd be more than happy to give our vehicle its next service. 'Our courtesy driver would be happy to drop you at home or at work when you leave your car with us.'

I was tempted to phone and get them to check our home address!

During our time in the nation's capital, we almost overdosed on Australian history, and while the tours of both Parliament Houses, old and new, were fascinating, and a visit to the National Library extremely exciting for me when I located my first book catalogued there, I was quite pleased to go along with Hon's suggestion of a drive around the plush suburb which housed the various embassies of the world.

We soon turned it into a game; who could pick the embassy merely from its architecture before we saw the identifying plaque. Most were easy. It was no surprise to realise the cold, modern lines of certain buildings housed embassies of the Scandinavian region, and the ornate, intricate carvings and pagoda-shaped roofs were for the Asian representatives. Most of the embassies were set behind large iron railings and patrolled by guards.

But suddenly Hon pulled up in front of one of the larger ornate buildings, and peered at the sign on the gate. 'Says they have daily tours between ten a.m. and four p.m. Let's take a look.'

Pressing the intercom button, we strained to understand the heavily accented voice echoing across the footpath. After asking if we could come in, the heavy grilled gate slowly swung open. The intercom crackled once more, and as the gate slammed shut behind us, we were told to enter a door to the side of the building. As we approached a counter fronted by a thick glass panel, I heard the reception door lock behind us, and a brown-faced man behind the glass beamed a white-toothed smile.

'Welcome to the embassy of Indonesia,' he said. 'Please to go through door and walk up steps. One of our staff, Yenny, she will greet you.'

Yenny stood at the top of the stairs, holding a large ring of keys and gracing us with her gentle smile. 'You are very welcome – please, if you would come in,' she said.

We entered a beautiful Balinese garden of lush green plants and trickling fountains in large ponds, and a feeling of peace immediately washed over me. Ushered through a heavily carved wooden door, we felt as though we were being invited into her home.

She moved with gentle rhythm, stopping at each beautifully displayed artefact, and sharing Indonesian history with us, her smile constant. We marvelled at the diversity of musical instruments, intricate handmade rugs and the complex detail of delicately sewn traditional costumes. Although she had lived in Australia for several years, Yenny's pride in her birthplace was evident.

I wanted to stay there, to drink in the peace and calm, but knowing she would never show any impatience to get back to work, I turned to her and smiled. 'Thank you so much, Yenny. We've never been to Indonesia but it looks such a beautiful place. Maybe we'll get there one day.'

Her look of almost pathetic gratefulness confused me, and her smile seemed sad.

'It is so nice of you to say these things,' she said. 'We have had many…' she paused, and seemed to be looking for the right word, 'not kind telephone calls recently,' she added. 'One of the gentlemen on the radio has given out our phone number asking people to ring and complain.'

I looked into her sad eyes, and suddenly realised what she was talking about. An Australian tourist had been caught with drugs at an Indonesian airport, and the Australian population was up in arms. The tourist was young, female and attractive, and media photos of her wide, startled eyes had attracted the indignation of Australians as they protested her innocence. And now another young and attractive girl, this one from Jakarta, was being caught up in the hysteria.

I squeezed her arm and murmured what I felt to be an inadequate thank you, and we patiently wended our way back through the security system.

Back at the motel, we talked about our insight into the world of one of our close geographical neighbours, and agreed it had helped dislodge the harsh scenes at the War Memorial the previous day.

Next morning I was reading *The Canberra Times* over breakfast, when a small news item caught my eye.

The Government has warned that death threats to the Indonesian embassy could harm accused drug smuggler Schapelle Corby's trial. The Indonesian Ambassador stated, 'We are getting quite a number of unaddressed, so to speak, emails, not only expressing their concern about the health, the condition, the legal proceedings on Corby, but as well threats.'

As we drove out of Canberra the next morning, I realised our country's capital had left two indelible impressions on me – one of pride and one of prejudice. The pride I felt for those young men and women who had fought so unselfishly so we could retain our freedom, but sadly, the prejudice that can change the face of one gentle girl with an infinite pride in her wonderful country.

23

When we left Canberra, it was only two hundred and fifty odd miles to the coast – not one of our more taxing days – but I was still surprised when Hon pulled over to the side of the road as we arrived in Goulburn.

'Why are we stopping? Bit early for coffee, isn't it?'

'You obviously didn't do your research on Goulburn very well. This, my mistress of massive monuments, is the home of the Big Merino.'

How could I have missed this one? It stands fifteen metres high, and when I compare all my 'big' photos, I have to admit this is my favourite. Maybe it's because I've always had a soft spot for the merino sheep, ever since a grade three project when I stuck cotton wool on a rather obese ovine my father drew, and received the top mark in the class. After we had 'snapped' one for the album, and one 'in case', we headed off once more. Kiama was calling, and sounded very appealing.

For the nature lover, there are walks along beautiful beaches around rocky outcrops and through lush rainforest, and if the more commercial aspect of the town appeals, there is a row of nineteenth-century terrace houses that has been converted into craft outlets.

But Hon found a different brochure the night before. 'You can do what you like in the bustling metropolis of Kiama, but I shall be visiting – and spending some considerable time, I might add – at the Kiama Blowhole!'

I just love it when he comes over all masterful. And just quietly, I was still experiencing a smidgeon of guilt over that other blowhole.

'This may come as a bit of a surprise,' I said, 'but I wouldn't mind seeing it myself.'

To say he nearly went into shock would be a serious understatement. Every piece of literature about the area mentions the famous Blowhole Point, and when I read that it attracts thousands of visitors each year,

I was ready to admit it must be fairly spectacular. Our usual routine on arriving in a town was to locate the caravan park and secure ourselves a spot as soon as possible. But not in Kiama! We could both hear the blowhole calling.

Blowholes occur when waves hit the rock formation at the edge of the sea, and spumes of water are shot high into the air. The water has been known to spray twenty-five metres into the air, but although the show was spectacular enough for us, it didn't quite reach such a great height. We weren't too disappointed, as apparently tourists on the paths get drenched when this occurs.

George Bass was the first white man to discover the blowhole in 1797, after hearing 'a most tremendous noise', and Kiama is named from an Aboriginal word meaning 'where the sea makes noise'. Still loving that native language! But it's not only the old history of the blowhole that is fascinating. In January 1889, a performer called Charles Jackson attracted large crowds when he crossed the mouth of the blowhole on a tightrope. Charles apparently made it safely over to the other side, but this tourist attraction is not without its tragic past.

As recently as 1992, seven people from two families were drowned when they were washed into the ocean by a wave while standing on the rocks. One of the bodies was never found, and there's a strange twist to this story. Five years later, the bodies of two cousins were found floating in the ocean off Kiama, and both girls were relatives of four of those who drowned in 1992.

Eventually, however, Hon decided that one could only marvel at the 'oomph' of water as it shoots into the air for a certain length of time, and anxious to settle ourselves in this very attractive coastal town, we headed for the Surf Beach Holiday Park. This is situated on a headland, and from the lawns at the front of the park, there is a wonderful view looking down on to the main beach.

I don't know what it is about the coast of New South Wales, but I saw so many places I could happily retire in, and Kiama was quickly added to this list. And when we heard that Thursday was not only schnitzel night but also meat market night (read 'meat tray raffle') at the Kiama Bowling and Recreation Club, we immediately felt at home.

Before I could say anything, Hon decided to take over the

pedestrian navigation that evening, and deduced the bowling club was only a ten-minute walk away. I swear, if we ever do this sort of holiday again, we're strapping pushbikes on to the back of the 'bago. That way, you can leave your van in the park, and still be mobile. Although when I mentioned this idea to Hon, he couldn't resist reminding me of my last cycling experience, when I started complaining after a mere five minutes of peddling!

'If we go to the end of this road, turn right then left, it's the next street on the right,' Hon announced, as we set off for the bowling club.

Well, we did all that – and it wasn't! We wandered and meandered for the next fifteen minutes until we turned a corner, and there it was.

'I knew it was round here somewhere,' Hon announced.

We both knew the discovery was more good luck than good management and he should have just left it at that – but no.

'Anyway, I've now shown you more of Kiama than you'd normally see, so that's been an added bonus.'

And that would be what? Fairly ordinary suburban streets with the minimum of lighting? Yeah – glad I didn't miss that!

But all was eventually forgiven, as we were welcomed inside the club and, in record time, served the most delightful home-made chicken schnitzel I have ever tasted. Tony, the CEO (I think it stands for Chicken Excellence Officer) of the club, proudly told me these schnitzels were famous around the country.

Hon breathed yet another sigh of relief as the meat raffle was drawn and I failed to find the winning ticket on the table in front of me. But I did think it was rather mean of him not to agree to another night in Kiama. On Fridays, they conduct a fish raffle, which comprises a selection of fresh local fish. I can almost understand his reluctance to carry round half a cow, but a few choice prawns – where would be the harm? With this sort of variety, I decided the blowhole was under serious threat as Kiama's main tourist attraction.

Batemans Bay is a popular resort with the people of Canberra. Only one hundred and forty-eight kilometres from the nation's inland capital, it's a perfect weekend getaway for landlocked lovers of ocean activities like fishing and sailing. Not only were there stunning views of mountains one way and an island dotted horizon the other, but National Geographic had listed it as one of the ten most clement climates in the world. You've got to love a place with that sort of credential!

We had made it a policy to select caravan parks by their close proximity to the town centre. We were not averse to exercise, as long as it did not entail carrying a compass and referring to an orienteering map. But at Batemans Bay, we deviated from this course. Once we set eyes on the Clyde View Caravan Park, we didn't care that it was three kilometres south of the town. It was perfectly located on the shores of Corrigans Beach, and there were enough shops at Batehaven to meet our needs.

Batemans Bay turned out to be a bit of a watershed for our relationship. Since Kiama, I was finally coming to grips with Hon's blowhole fetish, but this was only a small part of the problem. You see, my man was besotted with all brown signs – those guides to all attractions around the area. He found it physically impossible to drive past one with no other investigation than a mere glance, and if he wasn't on the lookout for blowholes, he was on the lookout for – well – lookouts!

There seemed to be an endless array of places where you could stand on a windy cliff and look out to yet another piece of ocean – which looked exactly the same as the previous piece of ocean. After lookout number one hundred and forty-three – well, it felt like that many – you needed a sharp knife to carve through the atmosphere inside the driving cabin. But at Batemans Bay, the tables were turned!

'Look, a zoo – they've got a zoo,' I shrieked. 'Back there – on the brown sign.'

Hon slowly pulled into the kerb, switched off the engine, and turned to me. 'Sorry, what was that? I don't think I heard you correctly. You've seen something on a brown sign you're excited about, is that right? Well, we'll just have to check it out, 'cause if it's important to you, darling, it's important to me.'

I think the grin that accompanied this statement was his undoing, but his left arm didn't bruise that badly, considering the force of the punch.

The privately owned Mogo Zoo is ten kilometres out of Batemans Bay. It is the only zoological park outside the larger public zoos that is dedicated to the conservation of exotic animals. The staff is committed to the survival of endangered animals, and provides world-standard facilities for over one hundred animals of more than thirty-eight rare species, including the only white lions in Australia. Their breeding record with snow leopards is particularly good, boasting two litters in the last three years. We ended up spending the whole day there, and even then it was hard for me to leave.

I could have dragged up a chair, and settled in for the day just to watch the meerkats. These appealing animals are part of the mongoose family, and have a unique personality, which is very endearing. Two facts about the appearance of these little guys fascinated me. The first thing you notice is a dark band around their eyes, and as this reduces glare from the sun, they have their own ready made 'set of shades'. They're also known as the solar panel of the animal world, because they expose their dark-skinned sparsely furred belly to the sun to warm up.

Meerkats live in a 'mob' and aside from being extremely sociable and communicative, also look out for each other. No matter what else is going on, there is always a sentry perched on top of the mound above the many tunnels, keeping a lookout for danger. It is this picture that always comes to mind when we hear the word 'meerkat', and although the photos of this habit always bring a smile to my face, it is even better to see the real thing. I was in my element, and Hon jokingly suggested leaving me at the meerkat enclosure while he continued the Winnie Wander, and then pick me up in a few weeks' time. (At least I think he was joking!) But it was feeding time for the Sumatran tigers, and not wanting to miss any part of this whole experience, I was happy to move on.

I've always believed animals have a sense of humour and the tigers at Mogo confirmed this theory. When the keeper introduced one of them to the crowd, the tiger strolled up to the bars, turned and showing us his rear end, proceeded to urinate in our direction. As this is a regular 'show of disdain' from this particular inhabitant, we had been warned to stand clear, but the crowd of tourists found it hysterical, and the tiger seemed satisfied with the audience reaction. But while that showed a certain intelligence, I was still puzzled as to why a large bowl inside the lions' cage had a sign above it reading 'Fresh Drinking Water'!

The snow leopard cubs were absolutely gorgeous and totally irresistible, and I was desperate to bring one home. Unfortunately I had to settle for the one that had magnets in all four paws, and now spends its day suspended from our stove range hood.

We had originally set aside a couple of days for Batemans Bay, as the zoo wasn't the only attraction close by. The historic mining town of Mogo had grown in popularity over the past ten years, and there are several historic buildings in the main street, with many of them housing shops featuring local arts and crafts. The original Mogo church with its pressed-tin walls is now home to a local south coast potter, and timber and leatherwork are other crafts available. But we were more interested in Old Mogo Town.

This is a reconstruction of a nineteenth-century gold rush village, and we decided to join one of the tours. The guide on this particular day was a font of knowledge, and his enthusiasm about the place was infectious. We had travelled around Tasmania several years earlier, and the stories of our convict settlement started our interest in Australian history. Add to this the tales of the early settlers on the mainland, and you start to understand how our nation was formed.

Fascinating as the tour was, I was anxious to utilise the small plastic phial we had been handed with our entry ticket. This was for the gold we were expected to find whilst panning at the old waterwheel. I was tempted to ask for a larger container – eternity ring size, perhaps – but no one else seemed dissatisfied.

Positioning myself around the edge of the cut down rainwater tank, I placed a scoopful of dirt and water into my tray. I had watched scenes of gold panning on movies and television, and had witnessed many 'eureka' moments. That's the one where the camera pans in on the pan and you see a minuscule amount of dirt and an even smaller amount of water, sitting at the base. On top of the dirt are flecks of gold, and the camera then moves to the broad grin on the prospector's face.

I carefully lowered the pan, scooped up some water, and swished it around. But all the dirt remained brown! And so I scooped and swished and rinsed, and scooped and swirled and swished again. (Yes, these are all official geological terms). Is there an expression 'he has the patience of a prospector'? If not, there should be. My hands were starting to resemble prunes and I was developing a miner's stoop (an acknowledged medical condition, I'm sure), when I thought I saw something glinting in the sun.

'Yes, yes, yes,' I squealed, doing my best *Harry Met Sally* impression. I licked the tip of my finger, dabbed it on the minuscule yellow spot, and dropped it into my phial of water. And that took precisely thirty-seven minutes! It was at that point I decided too much jewellery can look cheap.

I think they do Old Mogo Town a disservice calling it a 'theme park'. I'm the first one to admit the Queensland theme parks have a certain appeal, and we've spent a few fun days entertained in the world of dreams, dolphins and Disney. But thankfully, there are no screaming, gut-wrenching rides or excruciatingly happy 'characters' accosting you in the main street. This is a real look at our pioneer past, and thankfully they have not wrecked it.

24

I love cheese – all kinds! My perfect day would begin with a cheese omelette for breakfast, followed by cheese scones for morning tea, leading into a light, fluffy cheese soufflé for lunch. I would be quite happy to forgo an afternoon snack, so I was more than ready to nibble on cheese and garlic sticks with my pre-dinner drink. And then the *pièce de resistance* – dinner! A small serve of cheese and leek soup would allow ample room for the three-cheese sauce lasagne with lashings of parmigiana and, after an appropriate break, a fine slice of plain cheesecake. And there's nothing better to round off an evening than a nice cheese and fruit platter with your coffee.

My love of cheese started through another love – my grandfather. For the first twelve years of my life, he and Gran lived in a flat attached to the family home, and I worshipped the ground he trod.

George Rowland Weeks was a Yorkshire man, as round as he was tall, with a bald head ringed by a halo of grey hair, which I can still smell to this day, if I close my eyes, and the naughtiest blue eyes you could imagine.

Grandpa was a master storyteller, and I particularly loved hearing about his experiences in South Africa during the Boer War. He was a rider for Lord Kitchener, responsible for carrying messages to the front (and back). One day, as he was galloping through the jungle, his horse suddenly stopped, reared up and threw his rider to the ground. By the time Grandpa got to his feet, the large snake that was hanging from the branch of a tree overhanging the path had killed the horse. The snake's dimensions grew with each telling of the story, but I didn't care. I would be waiting for the ending, which always made me shiver.

'That beautiful boy saved my life, lass,' he would say, with tears in his eyes, 'and I'll never forget his sacrifice.'

This was the first time I would cry over an animal – I wish it had been the last.

But at other times, those naughty blue eyes would twinkle, when he related the story of where he spent his leave breaks. 'We'd go over to Paris and watch the girlies do the cancan.'

He'd roar with laughter at the memory and, young as I was, I knew I wasn't hearing the full story.

A few years later, I overheard him telling an old friend the same story, and adding the part that inspired such mirth. 'Not one of them wore panties!' he said, and the two old men had to prop each other up.

No wonder I loved this man! He adored animals and was never happier than when he was relating stories. And if that wasn't enough, his catchphrase 'don't tell your mother' would have ensured slavish adoration forever.

I was an extremely fussy eater as a child, and the worry of my mother's life. She would even serve my meal on a yellow plate, hoping the orange carrots, green peas and white potatoes would appeal to the aesthetics of my Libran nature, but to no avail. Meal times became a battle of wills, as I sat in front of my meat and three veg, with stony expression and tightly folded arms, with my mother refusing to allow me to leave the table until I had eaten the lot. I don't know why she bothered. Every family photo of me as a child, teenager and adult portrayed someone who was in no danger whatsoever of fading away!

But it wasn't the choice of meal that deterred me from the desire to dine. I couldn't fit another crumb in! To ensure that he would never lose his ample girth, Grandpa had a late afternoon snack every day, and I do use the word 'snack' loosely. It was identical to the meal they serve in hotels and call a ploughman's lunch. We would sit in the garden behind the orange tree, so Mum couldn't see us, and I would help grandpa eat chunks of crusty bread and crumbling cheese. I think he was secretly pleased I didn't fancy pickled onions and radishes too, as that left more for him. The food tasted even better because we were co-conspirators, hiding not only from Mum, but Gran as well.

My grandmother was a tiny little English rose with the appetite of a bird, and would often comment about Grandpa's girth. So with the wisdom husbands automatically acquire soon after the wedding ceremony, he realised life would be a lot more peaceful if Gran was kept in the dark about these 'high teas'.

I couldn't help thinking of this darling man as we approached the township of Bega, set in the lush pastures of the Bega Valley. Being prime dairy country and the rural centre of the Sapphire Coast, it has long been famous for Bega Cheese, and so a visit to the Bega Cheese Heritage Centre was a must.

I was looking forward to a factory tour, as I had fond memories of being shown around the Amscol ice cream factory when I was at primary school. The large machinery didn't do much for an eight-year-old, but the free samples went down a treat!

Unfortunately, because of strict OH&S food hygiene standards, factories around the country no longer conduct tours. I guess you don't want the general public sneezing over the Stilton.

The heritage centre is a reproduction of one of the first buildings to be built on the Bega Cheese factory site in 1899, and has a great display of cheese and butter making equipment from the early nineteenth century. We were just heading for the long counter where visitors are invited to taste the products available for sale, when a 'rumble of retirees' burst through the door, and made a surprisingly agile dash for the sampling area. Judging from the vast number, I assumed the latest tour bus had arrived. But before I could move to one side, I was snugly wedged between Joan and Bill, who were already conducting a critique of the produce.

'Try this one, Bill, love. It's nice and soft – think you'd probably call it a semi-matured.'

'You know I don't like cheeses that taste like a bar of soap, woman – give me something with a bit of bite.'

'Hey, Joan, have you tasted this one,' another woman yelled from further along the counter as she held a cube of cheese aloft on a toothpick, 'it's the Cheddar one.'

'No, dear,' said Joan, in a dulcet roar, 'they're all called Cheddar. That's probably the vintage. I've just given Bill a taste of the semi, but he doesn't like it. Can you toss us down a piece of the vintage, thanks, Merle? No, no – the one right in front of you, lovey.'

This went on for the next ten minutes and, unable to remove myself, I decided I might as well take advantage of the situation. I armed myself with a toothpick, ready to join in. But it seemed each time my sliver of wood headed towards a yellow cube, Joan or Bill or Ned or Fred or Wilma got there first. I began to suspect that the tour guide had announced there would be no time for lunch today so make the most of whatever you can find – and our septuagenarians certainly were.

I glanced around and gave Hon a cheesy smile, but then my grin broadened as I noticed the sign above the door, 'Bega Cheese Training Centre'. How fascinating! I wonder how long it took to train a cheese. Apart from telling them to 'sit', 'stay' and 'mature', I was struggling with the concept. Maybe I should guide our greedy grannies and grandpas over that way, and suggest they undergo some etiquette training – but maybe not. They already knew how to 'sit', they were prepared to 'stay' until the cheese disappeared, and the 'maturing' aspect had already taken care of itself. No, it was time to tuck the one-kilo block we had purchased under our arm and leave the dairy country to all those silly old moos.

When I first saw Merimbula, I thought of my school days. No, they weren't spent in a picturesque coastal village nestled between the mountains and the ocean with beautiful beaches and lakes. In my dreams! The reality was an old ivy-covered college in the heart of the Melbourne suburb of Kew where, from the minute I arrived each day, I was desperately waiting to leave.

There were only four things I enjoyed during my secondary schooling. The first were my friends, and these friendships have lasted through the years. The second was English class, the only lesson I really paid attention to, thanks to a brilliant teacher who made Shakespeare come alive for me. The third was drama club, although I still haven't forgiven them for casting me as Nanny, who happened to be a dog, when I auditioned for the role of Wendy in the school production of *Peter Pan*. And the final thing which made school worthwhile was the choir.

I will never forget the first time we were split into two groups, and my group was taught the descant of 'The Lord's My Shepherd'. The harmony seemed to flow through my body, and that hymn has always held a special place in my heart.

There was the less serious side to choir practice, one that the choir mistress wasn't privy to, of course. One of her favourite tunes was an Italian song written in 1880 called 'Funiculi Funicula'. It was inspired by the first funicular railway to be built on Mount Vesuvius – not that we girls could have given a toss – but I just loved the way the words rolled off my tongue. Aside from 'spaghetti' and 'Gina Lollobrigida', these were the only Italian words I knew at the time. There are only two lines I remember, but they were the most important anyway.

> 'Funiculi, funicula, funiculi, funiculaaaaaaaaaaaa
> Echoes sound afar, funiculi, funicula.

This had to be sung with the right hand extended high into the air. But I preferred my version.

> 'Merimbuli, Merimbula, Merimbuli, Merimbulaaaaaaaa
> I'ma sicka school, take me away in your sports car.

I had never been to Merimbula, didn't know anyone who had, and wasn't even sure exactly where it was. But I love words, and this one really appealed. I even had the whole scenario pictured in my mind. The sports car would be a powder-blue Austin Healey Sprite, and the driver was the head prefect at the boys' college up the road. My long blonde hair would fly behind me in the wind, as he gunned the accelerator and sped through the main street of Merimbula. Dressed in pale blue Bermuda shorts and top (to match the car, of course) I would be free at last from the confines of that 'ladies' college with their appalling school uniform of grey and bottle green.

Something went wrong with the dream, however, because here I was many years later, visiting Merimbula for the very first time. But I was driving down the main street in a white Winnebago, shouting instructions regarding the location of the caravan park, while my head prefect was getting snippy because I lost my place on the map! But all was soon forgotten, because I loved Merimbula, and couldn't agree more with the description of it as 'the jewel on the Sapphire coast'.

The Merimbula Holiday Park is situated in a lovely spot. No matter where you park, there are stunning beach and ocean views. We were beginning to see this whole trip as a reccie for further holidays, as yet again we had found another spot we could have settled in for several weeks. And something magical happened there as well; I found my inner Nigella Lawson. Being a short blonde, I'd long given up on the 'outer' Nigella.

On our tour around the township, we had called in to the Merimbula-Imlay Bowling Club, to see what time they started serving evening meals. The menu was very impressive, and I had already decided I would order 'beef eye fillet wiht (sic) grilled prawns'. But when we arrived back at the caravan park, there was a warm breeze, the sun glinted on the water and the seagulls were calling.

I turned to Hon. 'Let's stay in and cook – this is too nice to leave.'

A quick trip to the supermarket and a few hours later we were facing a dandy degustation of dynamic dimensions. It must have been just a touch of Merimbula magic, as, the minute we drove away from the town, my culinary skills deserted me.

There is no shortage of seafood restaurants in the town, and this is not really surprising – Merimbula has a reputation as a top fishing spot – but I did wonder how many people were put off by the name of one such establishment. It was called The Peppered Pelican! Most coastal towns we visited had their own colony of these majestic birds, and during the holiday, I had fallen in love with them (last photo count stood at seventeen). So the visual this name created was particularly horrific. Our feast at the caravan park did include a selection of the great local seafood, but all of it swam beneath the waves, not rode on top. If I had my way, the owner of that restaurant would have been severely assalted!

25

Many of the towns along the coast of New South Wales and Victoria have a history involving the whaling industry – the reason they were settled in the first place – and Eden is no exception. The town is situated at the southern end of the Sapphire Coast, and with the clear waters and sandy beaches of Twofold Bay to the east, forests and parklands to the west, and Mount Imlay in the background, this town has a rugged beauty all of its own.

The whaling industry of this region was started back in the early nineteenth century and went through till the 1920s, and the Eden Killer Whale Museum is a tribute to this history. The museum has been in operation over seventy years and is located on a hillside overlooking the Pacific Ocean. It houses many fascinating exhibitions, but none captured my attention and imagination, more than the story of Old Tom, a legendary killer whale of the district, who died in 1930.

Old Tom was an Orca, the species recognisable by their black and white markings, and he was the leader of a pack of Orcas who became known as the Killers of Eden. These Killers helped the whalers by spotting a lone whale and herding it into the bay so it would be easier for the whalers to catch. As a reward for this deed, the whalers would allow the Killers to feed on the whale tongues and lips, and as the tongues alone weighed up to four tons, it was an opportunity not to be overlooked!

If the Killers spotted a good whale to catch, and the whalers weren't working at the time, they would split the pod in two. Half the whales would go to the whaling station and slap their tails on the surface of the water; this being a signal to the whalers that there was something going on. The other half of the pod would already have started the slow process of killing the whale. Once the whale had been harpooned, the pod would help speed up the whale's death by swimming over the top of it, so it was unable to surface and take a breath, and then swim underneath to prevent it from diving deeper. Some of them would even throw their bodies over the whale's blowhole to stop it from breathing.

Surely the Judas of the animal world! Thankfully the last whale was taken in 1928, and although Eden is still famously associated with these magnificent mammals, it is merely a vantage point to watch the annual migration from Antarctica to the warm waters up north now.

Once I could drag myself away from this rather macabre tale, I wandered around the rest of the memorabilia in the museum. Apparently you can watch a gentleman called Phil McGrath send mores code messages to the HMB *Endeavour* every Wednesday, and from 1996 Phil was regularly communicating and plotting the *Endeavour*'s travels.

As we were visiting on a Monday, we didn't have the pleasure of Phil, but I noticed his chair is next to a sign that reads 'Please Touch With Eyes Only', so can only assume our Phil has a rather tactile fan base, which has probably become a tad tiresome.

There is a wonderful replica lighthouse, which is 'one of the original and traditional ones where keepers were in residence, before they were automated'. One would hope the lighthouses, not the keepers!

But as we walked outside three-quarters of an hour later, I knew which image would stay in my mind; the rather macabre tale of those 'blubbery bastard betrayers'.

A little known fact about Lakes Entrance is that on the first weekend in December, they hold the Tuggerah Lakes Mardi Gras festival, the highlight being the annual crowning of the Mardi Gras Queen. Now the big Mardi Gras parade in Sydney is around March each year, so this gives everyone plenty of time to get their frocks dry-cleaned and their leather nourished. And we're not talking some small rural pageant. It has been held for over fifty years, and is one of the largest parades outside of Sydney and Newcastle.

That's fascinating enough, but even the original history of Lakes Entrance is interesting. The first land grant made in the area known as Lakes Entrance, comprising one square mile, was promised to Henry Holden in 1828. However, he had some difficulty in taking possession. The authorities had made one of their many mistakes, and granted a lease of the area to Mr Bean (first name Willoughby), who was already in occupation. I could just picture the scene: Rowan Atkinson, in the 'too small' suit, clutching his mottled teddy bear, and sputtering with indignation through saliva-soaked lips, as Henry H demanded ownership.

The lease was eventually rescinded and Henry moved in. He named his small parcel of land Towoon, which is Aboriginal for the mating call of the wonga pigeon. (I couldn't help wondering what name Mr Bean would have used!)

I would imagine that was only the first of many arguments over land sales in this great place. I certainly wouldn't mind grabbing a plot of land here – but then there were so many places I was falling in love with, it would be difficult to decide on just one.

I'm sure you don't want to hear about yet another 'wonderful and picturesque coastal township with sun glinting on the blah de blah…' again. But as we drove out the next day, I couldn't resist winding down my window and yelling, 'WE'LL BE BACK!'

We needed to leave the main highway, for the next township we had been told to visit, and when we passed the Tambo River and drove through the rural pastures and lush rainforests, I suspected we would be glad we'd made this detour. And when we drove into the tiny village, saw the blue waters of the bay with feeding pelicans and small fishing boats, I was certain.

Metung is a tiny village set in the heart of the Gippsland Lakes, and has always attracted holidaymakers with its gentle ambience. As we sat on the lawns in front of the hotel, and looked across at the Moorings Resort, I was ready to ditch the 'bago and settle in here for at least two weeks.

The village is located on a thin strip of land which extends out into the Lakes, so with water on both sides, it's not surprising the main pastimes in Metung are fishing and boating. We spent several hours in this village with its laidback lifestyle, but after pigging out on lunch from the bakery, wandering in and out of the boutique shops along the main street, it was time to leave this 'peace' of tranquillity behind and rejoin the highway.

Inverloch should really be Lakes Entrance. Sure, they're roughly two hundred and fifty kilometres apart, but Inverloch is a Gaelic word meaning 'entrance to a lake'. That wasn't the most interesting thing I found out about this quiet little seaside resort, however.

Only forty-three kilometres out of Melbourne, Inverloch was a port used for the shipment of black coal, and a ship's carpenter, Martin Wyberg, achieved some notoriety when he disappeared from one of these ships, the *Avoca*, along with thousands of gold sovereigns from the ship's safe. Some of the sovereigns were later found at his home in Inverloch, so in an attempt to obtain leniency, he offered to lead the authorities to the rest of the cache, but escaped by overturning the police vessel in the Tarwin River. The district was searched, and even his house was demolished, but there was no sign of the lost sovereigns.

Some believe the treasure still remains in the vicinity; there is even a place called the Wyberg cave, near Walkerville, where the booty is supposedly stashed. As the last sighting of our wily carpenter was in Europe, my bet is the money travelled with him as well, but it's a part of the Inverloch legend, and makes a great story.

Judging from the amount of accommodation provided, the population of three thousand is boosted quite a bit during holiday periods. Thankfully, we were out of season, and the small township had a wonderfully lethargic feel to it.

We didn't visit it, but for those 'conchy' people out there, Jack Lewis has managed to amass one of the largest private shell collections.

When we left Inverloch the next morning, our plan was to drive directly to Sorrento. But I hadn't noticed how close we were to Phillip Island. Hon had never been there, and my only visit was with the family when I was twelve. We had just moved from Adelaide to Melbourne, because of Dad's job, and I was desperately missing my friends, particularly on the weekends.

Dad thought he had the solution. 'Let's go to Phillip Island, and stay till sunset so we can watch the penguin parade,' he announced.

Yes, a strange way to bolster a pre-pubescent female who just wanted to sit on the couch, wrapped in a mohair rug, eat four Kit Kats and watch Johnny O'Keefe on *Six O'clock Rock*. But I loved my darling dad, and was reluctant to hurt him, so agreed to go. And I was glad

I did! I've never forgotten the picture of all those little birds waiting in the shallows in their tuxedos, for the whole contingent, and then waddling up the beach, oblivious to the fascinated crowd.

As it was only ten a.m., Hon and I didn't think we'd wait around for a repeat performance all these years later, so decided to check out the other claim to fame this Victorian island boasts – the racing circuit. This is home to two big annual events – the Australian Motorcycle Grand Prix and the Superbike World Championship.

There is quite a comprehensive display in the foyer of the building at the track, which houses the history of motor racing, and I assume the place would be quite exciting for three days in October, when the air throbs with the sound of 500cc motorcycles. But on a weekday morning, with hardly anyone around, it didn't do much for my adrenalin. Still, we can now say 'I know where you're at' when a couple of rev-head friends of ours tell us they're heading to the island for the racing season.

26

When we first discussed this epic road trip, I naturally assumed all our travelling would be on roads, preferably highways. No, that's not quite true. I did allow for the occasional side road and, if there was something interesting at the end, even the odd bush track. That's the idea of a road trip, right? So I was a little surprised to hear Hon's suggestion.

'When we get to Sorrento, we can take the ferry across Port Phillip Bay to Queenscliff. It's only a forty-minute ride, and it'd be something different.'

Sounds pleasant, I hear you say? Well, yes – If you like being away from solid ground with twenty thousand leagues of forbidding ocean directly under your feet. And I don't! I looked up from the brochure I was studying and couldn't mistake the look of excitement on my man's face. While he was aware of my hesitancy regarding all things floating, I think he was hoping I would take this opportunity to meet a personal challenge.

'Yes – as you say – different,' I mumbled.

He must have interpreted this comment as unbridled enthusiasm, because here we were in Sorrento, and he had just purchased a ticket for the next crossing.

Sorrento is a seaside village situated on the Mornington Peninsula and one and half hours out of Melbourne. Many of the buildings date back to the nineteenth century and are made of local quarried limestone. This was the sight of the state's first settlement in 1803, thirty years before the founding of Melbourne, but was short-lived due to the lack of freshwater resources.

The front beach is an ideal place to picnic, take a swim or keep watch for bottlenose dolphins, but the back beach on the Bass Strait side of the peninsula attracts serious surfers. As well as a large assortment of shops along Ocean Beach Road offering everything from boutique clothing to jewellery and artwork, they have a great choice of eateries.

Although the ferry departed on the hour every hour, we had just managed to miss one, so decided to grab some lunch.

The Hotel Sorrento was built in 1871 and was the first established business in Sorrento. It is now a four and a half star establishment with very modern dining facilities and luxury accommodation. We had just perched on the high backless stools and found a few centimetres of space to accommodate our lunch on the small round table, when a piercing voice interrupted the seaside ambiance.

'Oh God, look at me. I look fraightful!'

Given an invitation like that, I couldn't resist, so glanced across at the two women sitting at one of the window tables. They both appeared to be approaching forty, albeit from the wrong side, and were dressed in understated couture which subtly murmured 'old money'. Unfortunately, the bling dripping from their fingers, ears and throats screamed 'nouveau riche'. The 'voice' was grimacing at the reflection of her sunburnt face in a small compact mirror.

'James goes on incessantly about the money ai spend at the salon, but if this is doing it naturally, I'll stay with the spray,' Sweetie said.

Her friend swept French-manicured fingertips through her subtly streaked bob. 'This whole day's been a complete disaaaster. Why the boys can't be satisfied going out in the cruiser, ai don't know – at least it has a covered deck. Let's make it perfectly clear next time they want to go fishing in that ghastly little thing that we're not prepared to play Becky Thatcher to their Huckleberry Finn,' Darling said.

Sweetie let out a staccato noise I assumed was mirth. 'How brill – must remember that one. Ai don't think it'll be a prob – everything's a one-minute wonder with those two. What about those jet skis they just haaaad to have last summer? How many times did they end up using them – was it four? And then they were put away!'

She finished surveying the sun damage to her face and poured another glass of bubbles. 'Wouldn't it be simply divaine if we could go to Thredbo by ourselves next year? I'd even learn how to put the chains on the car if I had to!'

Suddenly I felt a tap on my arm, and turned to see Hon smiling.

'Enjoying the conversation, are we?' He looked at his watch. 'Think we better head off. The ferry's due to leave soon.'

Although the women's situation failed to engender any sympathy from me, I couldn't resist handing out some advice, as we passed their table. 'Have you got any tomatoes?' I asked.

They synchronised their withering looks perfectly, as their brains assessed the cost of my outfit, and came up wanting.

'It takes the sting out of the burns,' I said, smiling sweetly.

'Haven't got a remedy for being a total twit, however,' I was tempted to add.

There was a moment of awkwardness as they decided whether I was worth the effort.

'That's soooo kaind of you – thaaaanks,' said Sweetie, trying to affect a smile, but failing.

As we left the hotel, I heard Darling say to Sweetie (or maybe it was the other way round – who cares?), 'Do we know her?' and the response of 'Hardly' spoke volumes.

The ferry was a sleek affair and apparently had the capacity for eighty vehicles and seven hundred passengers. We would be travelling at eleven knots, but as my nautical information was pretty much non-existent, I was unsure whether this meant we would be skimming across the top of the waves or merely chugging along fractionally faster than a rowboat. Although the brochure mentioned the ferry was purpose built to be unaffected by rough weather and the service had never been cancelled in eighteen years, this did nothing to increase my confidence in the exercise of leaving dry land. I had visions of black clouds looming over the horizon, lightning flashes zapping restless waves and thunder claps loud enough to deafen. I could even imagine the conversation on the bridge.

> 1st Mate: Do you think we should take her out today, sir? There's quite a storm brewing. Doesn't look as if we'll make it across to the other side before it hits.
>
> Captain: No, you're probably right – but I'm not about to break the eighteen-year record. If we have to go down trying, then so be it.

After parking amongst the other vehicles in the cargo hold, we made our way to the upper deck, and I was pleasantly surprised to find a carpeted lounge area, with comfortable seating and a large-screen television. I felt so brave, actually being on board this floating deathtrap, but it didn't mean I wanted to stand and watch the land recede further and further into the distance. I walked over to the sofa and settled back for a dose of daytime entertainment.

'On your best day, young man, you're not half as clever as me on my worst day,' yelled Judge Judy. Her voice seemed to resonate around the whole area, as she addressed the poor hapless youth standing before her.

He opened his mouth, but before any words could escape, the Judge was ready. 'And don't pee on my leg and tell me it's raining, all right?'

As the gallery of the courtroom dissolved into laughter, the young black dude still felt he needed to justify his case. 'But, your honour, me and my bro, we was not there.' He pointed to a guy slouching in a chair to his left. 'You aks him – he tell you da troof.'

'Not interested. I don't need to "aks" him – I don't even want to ask him – do you hear me?' Jude replied. 'You two have probably got more stories than Damon Runyan!'

I laughed, and glanced at the elderly woman sitting next to me. 'I'd hate to come across her in a courtroom,' I said.

She threw me a nervous smile. 'At least it'd be on dry land. I hate boats.' Her hand shot out and grabbed my arm. 'You hear about accidents with these things all the time. They overload them then they sink!'

Although she was slightly built, her grip was surprisingly firm. Great! Out of all the people I could have sat next to!

'That sort of thing doesn't happen here in Australia,' I said. 'That's more around Asia, where their regulations are not as strict.' Why was my voice so loud?

Her grip tightened. 'But I can't swim, dear.'

I suddenly had a terrifying vision. The ferry is doing a nosedive into the briny (*Titanic*-style) and this woman's death grip is dragging me to a watery grave. I glanced through the window and noticed Hon standing on deck. This had to be the lesser of two evils.

'It's a bit stuffy in here,' I said, my voice a whisper now. 'Think I'll go out on deck for a while.'

The woman's eyes widened. 'You go careful, dear. If you fell overboard, you wouldn't stand a chance with those propellers.'

Hon looked up in surprise as I burst through the doors and joined him at the railing. He draped his arm round my shoulder, and gave me an encouraging smile, convinced I'd decided to face my demons.

'Smell the sea air. Isn't it great?' he said.

Yes, beats the smell of fear from inside the ferry!

'We should be landing fairly soon. I'm pretty sure they'll pull in over there,' he said, indicating a small jetty.

My heart palpitations started to subside. We were nearly there – I'd done it! I was so pleased with myself. This is what holidays are all about; opening yourself up to different experiences. And then the engine stopped!

My relaxed demeanour vanished in that split second, and I grabbed Hon's arm. 'What's happening? Why are we stopping? You said we'd be landing shortly – what are they doing?' I didn't need a mirror to know my pupils had dilated dangerously. 'I – need – to – get – off – now,' I enunciated carefully, just in case he missed the message from the eyes.

But before he could even open his mouth to calm my fears, the man on my other side was addressing me.

'Looks like they've run out of fuel. There's no way you can get off. We'll probably be stuck here for hours.'

My head whipped around and I glared at the speaker leaning casually against the railing. 'Please don't say that. I'm not a good traveller and I'm feeling really nervous at the moment.'

He looked me up and down and snorted. 'You're all the same, you bloody women. Have to be in control all the time. Just as well my wife's at home – she'd be whingeing about the same bloody thing! Well, there's nothing you can do about this, lady – you're stuck here – so you're just gonna have to like it or lump it.'

A statement such as this would usually exacerbate any panic I was feeling, and unless you have experienced one of these attacks, it is difficult to explain. But noticing the pleasure this man was deriving from my terror, it suddenly had the opposite effect. No way was I giving him the satisfaction of showing how much his words had upset me. I squeezed Hon's arm and indicated I would sit on one of the benches surrounding the deck.

I think the ferry remained motionless for about twenty minutes – I couldn't be sure of the exact time, I was too busy with pad and pencil, writing a story about the perfect murder. It took place on a ferry similar to the one we were on. Let me explain.

> There was a dull thud as the ferry made contact with the wharf. The large door of the cargo hold slowly lowered to form a ramp between the ferry and the jetty. Suddenly there was a muted rumble as the drivers turned on their engines. Two deck hands stood either side of the ramp as the vehicles started to exit the hold, but as usual the transition from sea to land was smooth, and the men had little to do. After they had watched what they thought was the last car drive up the ramp, one of the deckhands glanced into the hold, and frowned.
>
> 'Hey, Jack, there's still one left,' he yelled.
>
> Jack wandered over to the solitary car, but there was no one inside. 'I better go and see if he's fallen asleep somewhere and missed the call.'
>
> Half an hour later all six deckhands had completed a thorough search, but there was no trace of the driver. The local police were notified, and the vehicle removed from the ferry.
>
> Jack never gave it another thought – that was, until the following week, when he noticed a small item in the local newspaper.
>
>> Joggers discovered the body of a man on a Mornington Peninsula beach at 5.45 am yesterday. While a post-mortem examination to officially determine how the man died will be carried out, initial inquiries indicate the circumstances surrounding his death are not suspicious. Although formal identification has yet to be finalised, initial reports indicate this could be the man who disappeared from the Queenscliff ferry several days ago.
>
> Several hundred kilometres away, a woman was reading the same news item. After finishing, she placed the newspaper in her lap, leant back in her deck chair, and gazed around the caravan park.
>
> 'Looks like another lovely day,' she said, smiling at her husband. 'What about a round of golf, darling?'
>
> Those lessons and practice sessions at the driving range had certainly built up her upper body strength. Being only 147cm tall and tipping

the scales at 52kg, people were often fooled into believing she needed looking after. But anyone who crossed her soon regretted it. She glanced at the paper once again and a smile creased the corners of her mouth. It was amazing how her boating phobia had been cured so completely!

27

Queenscliff is one of those delightful seaside resort towns which is both a popular beach-side destination and a sophisticated retreat with elegant hotels, guest houses and galleries. It is situated on an isthmus (probably a peninsula, but I just love that word) at the south-eastern tip of the Bellarine Peninsula, just inside the entrance to Port Phillip Bay.

The Wathawurung Aborigines, who befriended a white man, William Buckley in 1803, originally inhabited the area. William was a convict who escaped when a party under the command of Lieutenant Governor Collins established a settlement at Point King. Buckley married a woman of the tribe and they had one daughter and lived in the area for thirty-two years, before William decided to rejoin European civilisation. I'd love to have known why he decided to leave the tribe after all that time, but the reason is not recorded.

The township was originally called Whale Head when it was established in 1836, but was renamed Shortland Bluff soon after. In 1853, Governor Charles La Trobe renamed the townsite Queenscliff, in honour of Queen Victoria. Perhaps the gentry of that period felt it a tad common to say their summer holidays would be spent at Whale Head!

There is a fascinating legend about the area. In 1798, a pirate named Benito Benita (what were his parents thinking?) buried plundered Spanish treasure in a cave in the cliffs of Swan Bay. Benita was caught in the act by the British navy, and sealed the cave entrance with gunpowder. He was caught and hanged, while his cabin boy, who was supposedly tattooed with the map showing the exact location of the treasure, lay low in Tasmania. This lad is said to have returned to spend his last years in Queenscliff, presumably without consulting the map on his body.

What a wonderfully romantic tale – and what a crock, I say! If our little cabin boy was going to endure the pain of having a bleeding great map tattooed on his body, wouldn't he go back to the cave later on, take the Spanish treasure, and 'see you later, alligator'? Anyway, no official record of Benita's capture exists, and part of this alleged treasure, the statues from a cathedral in Peru, can still be found in the aforementioned cathedral! Various syndicates and individuals have undertaken serious excavation work in search of the treasure, and I'm sure you'll be as surprised as I was to hear that none have been located!

And if that wasn't enough to put Queenscliff on the map, there was the story about the famous Australian painter, Sidney Nolan. He and his friend stowed away on a ship in Melbourne in 1934, hoping they could get a free passage to France, but were discovered even before the ship left Port Phillip, and thrown in the Queenscliff gaol. The plan was to pass themselves off as missionaries, but they had obviously failed to think this one through. Neither of them had a working or even idle knowledge of the Bible, and the prospect of being teetotal for the entire trip sent the lads weak at the knees.

It was tempting to hang around this pretty town steeped in such colourful history, but our next accommodation waited at Daylesford, and we planned on visiting Torquay on the way.

This section of the Great Ocean Road is known as the Surf Coast, and with two of the nation's best surf beaches, Bells and Jan Juc, at the front doorstep, it was inevitable that Torquay would emerge as one of the state's most popular surfing locations. As usual, we headed straight for the 'You Are Here' centre, but we were not after information; this is the home of the famous Surfworld Museum.

Although I couldn't lay claim to owning a surfboard during my teenage years (a black rubber mattress when I was ten years old was the best I could come up with), I did attend dances at the local surf club in my teenage years, and was nicknamed Gidget, after the 1959 movie starring Sandra Dee and James Darren. I'd love to say it was because I was as cute as Sandra Dee, but suspected it was more because I fitted the description of 'girl midget'.

The Surf Museum is a remarkable tribute to surfing through the ages. The first thing I noticed was a giant surfboard containing hundreds of signatures. It served as a memorial to Australia Day 2005, when five hundred surfers paddled out and formed a huge circle. This was a tribute to the many people lost or devastated by the Asian tsunami disaster, and each participant had signed the board.

The history of this sport is fascinating. An Hawaiian man with the very impressive moniker of Duke Kahanamoku introduced surfboard riding to Australia on 15 January 1915 at Freshwater Beach, New South Wales. At that stage surfers were using hollow plywood boards up to eighteen feet long and it wasn't until 1956, when a visiting US lifeguard team introduced Australians to the balsa/fibreglass Malibu style board, that surfing was revolutionised.

In a small side room, they run continuous surf movies, both past and present, and it depicts very clearly the danger these surfers face. I was convinced this was a young person's game, even before I read the sign next to the Surfing Fitness and Aerobic Paddling test, which suggested, 'People over 35 years of age should not undertake this test.'

We were so caught up reading about the history of the sport, we didn't realise it was getting late, so only had time for a quick drive past Bell's Beach, to see four surfers resembling small dots in the vastness of the ocean battling reasonable-size waves, before we headed inland.

28

When we looked at our travels on the map so far, it was a twisted, but fortunately not bitter line we were drawing around the three states and one territory of Australia we had covered so far. Having reached the beginning of the scenic drive along the Great Ocean Road, you may wonder why we were suddenly headed north away from the coast, to a town set in the mountains one hundred and ten kilometres north of Melbourne.

Daylesford and the adjoining town of Hepburn Springs are regarded as the spa centres of Australia, and boast fifty per cent of the nation's known mineral springs. This in itself would be enough reason to make the diversion, but there was another much more important draw card. I lived in Melbourne most of my teenage years and formed some true friendships in that time and, although we had lived in separate states for many years, those friendships were still strong.

A couple of years ago, my school friend Lizzie and her partner Graham, had purchased a weekender in Lauriston, a small hamlet twenty-seven kilometres outside Daylesford, and when she realised we would be in the area – to Lizzie that meant anywhere in Victoria! – she insisted we visit. We didn't need coaxing. But before they arrived from Melbourne for the weekend, we had a couple of days by ourselves to explore the surrounding area.

Daylesford is the home of Michael Leunig, who is not only well known through his cartoons which appear in the Melbourne *Age* and occasionally the *Sydney Morning Herald*, but also through a number of books centred on the strange figure with the unusual cranial features. He has been called an observer, a philosopher, a dysfunctional genius and a catalyst for free thinking, but my favourite title is 'historian of the absurd'. I can really relate to a person who writes a book titled *The Adventures of Vasco Pyjama*!

As we walked down the main street of Daylesford, I was taken back to the late sixties and seventies when the new kids on the block, the hippies, were embracing an alternative lifestyle. But unlike Byron Bay, where all this seemed artificial and contrived, Daylesford is the real thing, and you found yourself wanting to experience it all.

There are many businesses offering all sorts of 'alternative' services, and these include reiki, shiatsu, acupuncture, aromatherapy, reflexology, spiritual healing and tarot and psychic readings. I had been so impressed with my 'fizzik' reading at the Crystal Castle that I couldn't wait to compare notes with another clairvoyant. But this one turned out to be a 'chrisvoyant' filling in for his wife, and either he was full of it or my vibrations were not trembling correctly that day.

There are plenty of suggestions to keep you busy around the area, including a rather unusual suggestion to 'take a llama to lunch'. Sounded interesting, and probably wouldn't be that expensive. After all, how much can a llama eat? But then it was explained what this entailed, and although it was tempting to follow one of these cute South American animals up a hill, carrying my gourmet lunch on its back, we had to say 'no' – there were higher priorities.

Both Daylesford and Hepburn Springs are famous for the odourless, effervescent mineral water emanating from the many springs in the area. The towns are located on top of rock strata and volcanic basins, and waters trapped in these basins have slowly leached minerals from four hundred and fifty million year old rocks. These minerals are believed to have a curative effect, and are the basis of both towns' existence. The area fell out of favour in the Great Depression, but since the early 1980s, interest in the local waters has revived and, along with many tourists, the town's fortunes have been rejuvenated.

Daylesford was originally named Wombat, but then sensibly renamed by Sir Charles Hotham, after the English birthplace of Warren Hastings, the first governor-general of India. Good move, I say. Can you imagine telling your friends you were going away for the weekend?

'Great – where are you off to?'

'Oh, just going to take the Wombat waters.'

My friends would take the piss!

Hepburn Spa is situated in a very pretty wooded setting, and I felt relaxed the minute we walked up to the Reception area. We had booked for a private spa in the invigorating mineral waters, followed by a one-hour massage. We checked in and were handed a white bathrobe each, and told to change.

'When you're ready, please come and sit in the lounge area, and one of our staff will come and get you.'

Five minutes later we were sitting in a room full of strangers, trying to look as though we always went out in public in our dressing gowns, while making sure the two pieces of material in the front didn't part company!

The obligatory piddling fountain to enhance relaxation was bubbling away in the corner, the aroma of sandalwood filled the air and I was already feeling the recuperative powers of the spa. But then a woman approached the counter, requesting a replacement for her wet robe.

'Sorry, we only give out one robe,' the receptionist said.

I glanced at the woman sitting next to me, hoping she had a firm grip on the latte she was sipping.

As we were shown into a small bathroom which had been built around the turn of the twentieth century and untouched since, all visions of your pristine porcelain palace fled out of the small window high up on the wall. We stripped and tentatively lowered ourselves into the warm shallow liquid, which resembled water from a kitchen sink in a busy restaurant.

'You realise our bodies are going to be rejuvenated only from the waist down and our chest and head will still be the same age!' I said to Hon.

I've got to be honest. It wasn't the most exciting experience I've had in a tub – that one I'm saving for the next book – but then came the massage! This can be done *à deux*, and after drying ourselves and throwing on the still dry towelling gowns, we were directed to another room. A lovely young girl was waiting for me, and a fit young guy was ready for Hon, who was convinced they had the configuration wrong, although it suited me fine!

Not sure of the protocol in these situations, I figured they'd 'seen it all before', so threw my gown off and hopped onto the table.

'Oh, we usually go out while you get yourself comfortable on the table – most people like a bit of privacy. Oh well, it doesn't matter now,' said my masseuse.

Oops! I was left with the clear understanding that it would be better to act like 'most people' next time, and I discovered it's possible to blush all over. But then all was forgotten, and I was transported to heaven.

I don't want to be disloyal to my angel at Crystal Castle, but I think this massage probably rated one star higher. Certainly that's where I was heading as those magic fingers kneaded me, and from a couple of satisfied grunts emanating from the next table, Hon felt the same. When we walked through the door on jelly legs an hour later, we decided a future visit would be a great idea.

And now it was time to catch up with Lizzie and Graham – I was so excited! From the moment we finalised our plans, our hostess was adamant.

'It's a very ordinary house – please don't expect too much – it's back to basics.'

So as we drove up to the quaint weatherboard cottage with surrounding veranda, set on three acres of ground, which included dams, a river and a creek, I decided immediately that 'getting back to basics' was going to be just my thing. And if the glorious view over the peaceful countryside wasn't enough, the inside of this weekender was just as delightful. Lizzie has always displayed a strong creative streak, and it was the perfect rustic retreat.

There were floor to ceiling picture windows in the large family room, affording an ever-changing vista of the property, if you could take your eyes away from the inner surroundings. A profusion of wild flowers had been placed around the room in an eclectic bunch of containers, and jam jars were filled with berries and twigs and branches of small wild apples. An unusual and unique collection of small bottles had been arranged along the windowsill, and each one had been found on the property. Even the dressmaker's dummy standing in the corner added a wonderfully personal touch, as it belonged to Lizzie's mother when she was twenty, and was the template for many glorious outfits. Although our host and hostess were suitably impressed with our gal Winnie, they were quick to spot the rather cramped sleeping arrangements, and insisted we take over the guest bedroom for the next couple of nights. We didn't need to be asked twice!

After we had settled in, there were drinks on the veranda and, being early evening, the bird life was prolific. The wrens, robin red breasts, parakeets and many others were always made welcome, but not the cockies. These were the villains and varmints of the ornithological world, as far as country folk were concerned, as they were rather partial to the wooden veranda posts and window ledges of houses. Being fairly new tree changers, our friends had listened intently to every piece of advice regarding this problem from 'them what were in the know'. So our evening drinks were taken amongst several plastic snakes along the balustrade, a wooden crow and wooden owl hanging from pieces of fishing line, and sundry bits of black tape which hummed in the wind. But alas, the boids had seen it all before, and were unmoved!

As night descended, the silence hung like a thick velvet blanket and the temperature dropped rapidly, so we moved inside. There was an open fire, which filled the room not only with welcome warmth, but the redolent aroma of the lavender and pinecones which had been placed amongst the wood. I'm not sure whether it was the cosy atmosphere, a beautiful meal or the fresh country air, but we were soon heading off to bed.

The first thing I was aware of when I opened my eyes the next morning was the deafening sounds of silence. Living on a busy suburban street, we were used to the whoosh of passing traffic. And it can be just as difficult to sleep when this is absent. But I didn't mind. I wasn't about to miss a moment of this weekend, and when I pulled the curtain back I wished I could be greeted with this scene every morning. The eerie mountain mist sat low across the valley, brushing the tops of the gum trees with a white powder coating. Two adult kangaroos approached the edge of the dam to take their first drink of the morning, and as one of them bent down, a joey's head appeared from the pouch, followed quickly by the rest of the small body. And I envied sea changers!

The next two days were one of the highlights of our holiday. Lizzie and I managed to grab some valuable girl time, and wondered more than once what age we would be when we finally grew up. The boys amused themselves down by the dam with rods and bait, but we secretly didn't have high expectations of them furnishing us with a trout dinner.

Yes, there's a lot to be said for this life of ride-on mowers, brush cutters, gumboots by the back door, hats you wouldn't be seen dead in back in the big smoke and yes, even the wood pile with spiders the size of saucers. I won't be surprised to hear that our friends have truly embraced nature and made this their permanent address in a few years' time.

29

As we were nearing the end of our holiday, the most logical route to take when we left Lauriston was down to Ballarat, join the Western Highway and travel through Bordertown, Keith, Tailem Bend, Murray Bridge and finally Adelaide. I'm fairly safe in saying there would be little or no chance of encountering delays through blowhole viewings so this route had a certain appeal – for me anyway. But this was not the route we chose. When one of the world's leading travel magazines puts a trip along the Great Ocean Road in the top twenty journeys of a lifetime, we felt compelled to finish the trip we had started before veering off inland, a few days earlier.

As soon as we left the mountain countryside around Daylesford and Hepburn Springs, we were totally focused on reaching the coast once again, and although our journey took us through Ballarat, Cressy and Colac, apart from a refreshment and fuel stop, we covered the two hundred and fifty kilometres to Apollo Bay in record time.

Similar to the New South Wales coastal towns, many of their Victorian counterparts started life as whaling stations, and Apollo Bay was no exception. It has a holiday atmosphere, even though we were there outside the high season, and because the weather was unseasonably warm, we didn't find it difficult to hang around for a couple of days.

On the second night, we decided to treat ourselves to a slap up meal. My touch of the Nigellas had disappeared almost overnight, so we made a booking at a restaurant up the road from the caravan park, with a tempting menu in the window. And not only did the food turn out to be top class, but the wine as well. We lingered over a bottle of Verdelho, ordered a second liqueur and, when the staff started sweeping under our legs, realised the evening was drawing to a close.

I'd like it to go on record that, up to that moment, I was making perfect sense. We had spent the time over dinner reviewing our holiday, and planning the next one, and anyone knows you have to have your marbles about you for that. But then we opened the front door of the restaurant, stepped onto the pavement, and the cool night air slapped me across the face. I turned to Hon, to make a profound statement, about – something – but instead, collapsed onto the nature strip, laughing so much, the tears ran down my legs! Hon joined in – the laughter, not the tears – and helped me adopt an upright position, but I had only taken three steps, when the nature strip became irresistible once more.

I put my hands up to my face. 'Have I got chushed fleeks?' I asked, enunciating quite beautifully.

Hon grinned. 'Not just your fleeks – everything else too. Think you better hop on,' he said, squatting down and offering his back, 'otherwise we'll never get you back to the park.'

And so I was ceremoniously piggybacked down the main street by my 'shite in ironing armour', as I dubbed him, and fell into the second stupor of the trip.

I know what you're thinking. Surely she learnt her lesson after the Hunter Valley episode! But this was entirely different. I'm convinced I picked up a seafood allergy that night, and it obviously went straight to my head!

Hon was sorry to leave Apollo Bay the next morning. He felt it was a top spot for a holiday. I was sorry to leave my bed, let alone Apollo Bay, as every slight movement became a challenge. But then the drugs kicked in. After I'd washed a couple of paracetamol down my throat with a dose of caffeine, I felt ready for anything. Well, anything that didn't have alcohol as an ingredient!

The Great Ocean Road stretches for three hundred kilometres along Victoria's south-west coast, from Torquay to Warrnambool. The road was built between 1919 and 1932, and can probably lay claim to being the biggest war memorial around. It was constructed by returned servicemen, using only picks and shovels, and is dedicated to all those who fought in the First World War.

This winding coastal road seems to change constantly. At times you are teased with fleeting glimpses of the ocean through the dense saltbush, then suddenly the landscape opens up, and you are travelling next to the ocean. The colours are magnificent, as the pale aqua of the water close to shore abruptly changes to a deep ink navy, making a dramatic contrast with the ochre-coloured cliffs on the right. In certain areas we felt we were hovering on a ledge between the cliff and the coast, but by this stage, I had enough faith in the 'bago's ability I was able to relax and enjoy the visual delights while inhaling the salty smell of the sea through the open window. In other parts of the road you climb high into the mountains, finally emerging to look down on the rugged coastline, but then the road quickly drops, and the coast is within touching distance on your left once more.

As we approached the rugged coast near Cape Otway, it was not hard to understand why this is known as the Shipwreck Coast, a place where a hundred and eighty ships came to grief in the nineteenth century. It was the first sign of land for ships sailing from Europe and America, and Matthew Flinders seems to say it all: 'I have seldom seen a more fearful section of the coastline.'

The one detail most people know about the Great Ocean Road is one of the must see attractions called the Twelve Apostles. This is a collection of rock sculptures formed by erosion of the original coastline. The action of the sea on the limestone slowly wore down the rocky cliff, eventually leaving individual rocks. The cliff is still being eroded at a rate of about two centimetres each year, and in the future, is likely to form more 'apostles'. It's impossible to see all of them from the lookout; the others are hidden behind the headlands or other outcrops. It's really an area of changing scenery, as a number have collapsed over the years, so perhaps they should have been more vague about the number and stuck to the original name Sow and Piglets. The Sow was Muttonbird Island and the piglets were the smaller surrounding rocks.

We did find ourselves another blowhole, and this one came with an interesting story. It was connected to the sea by a long narrow tunnel, and when heavy seas are running, waves compress air trapped in the tunnel, and enter the cavern. The tunnel of the blowhole extends a hundred metres inland, and is gradually being enlarged by the force of the sea. Hon was almost euphoric! After the wreck of the ship *Loch Ard*, the waters of the blowhole situated at Loch Ard Gorge glowed with an eerie purple light, which came from phosphorous matches washed in from the cargo.

Most of the people on board died that night, but two of the passengers did survive. A young girl named Eva Carmichael, who was only eighteen, had clung to some wreckage and finally drifted close to shore in a small bay. Too exhausted to make it on to the beach, she was ready to collapse, but fortunately a lad named Tom Pearce, who happened to be the same age, witnessed her struggle and swam out to rescue her. And she immediately fell in love with her hero, they married and had a long, happy life together. Wrong! Although Tom and Eva were the only survivors from the wreck, Eva ended up going back to Ireland three months later, and Tom married a woman who was related to a man who died in the shipwreck.

30

For such a quaintly named township, Port Fairy has a less than attractive history. A whaling station was set up in 1835, but so many of the Southern Right Whales were taken from the area that the East Beach was littered with their bones. These were eventually collected, ground to powder and used for fertiliser. By 1845, the supply of whales was exhausted and the whaling station closed, but fortunately the surrounding land was rich in opportunities, and three men, Griffiths, Mills and Campbell, brought sheep and cattle from Van Diemen's Land. This turned out to be a bold move as the government of NSW was not yet ready to grant legal title to land in this remote corner of this colony.

A town called Belfast was established, although the harbour was always known as Port Fairy, and over the next fifteen years many settlers were attracted to the area. The population increased rapidly and by 1857, 2,190 people lived in one of the most flourishing towns in the new Colony of Victoria. Then the local import firm crashed in 1900, there was little economic development. Fortunately, many of the old buildings still stand which means there is a rich variety of architecture in Port Fairy.

The Belfast Cove Caravan Park is advertised as a 'boutique' park (tourist talk for 'small') but the sites are set in a beautiful garden surrounded by cypress hedges, and because each site is bordered on three sides by shrubs and flowers, you can be assured of privacy. Win seemed more than pleased with her ambient surroundings, so we headed off for a stroll around this pretty port.

As we wandered streets lined with massive Norfolk pines and past nineteenth-century whitewashed whalers' cottages, Georgian-style merchants' homes and old stone churches, it didn't take much imagination to visualise what Port Fairy would have been like a hundred years ago.

The Caledonian Inn (the locals call it 'the Stump') was established in 1844 and is the oldest continually licensed hotel in Victoria. And the wording is specific, because it's not the oldest hotel! That title goes to the Merrijig Inn, which dates back to 1841. While the Stump has always served as a hotel, the Merrijig has had a colourful history. It also served as a meeting room for the council, performed the duties of the local courthouse, and at one stage was even the police barracks. The history relating to the barracks made me smile.

The police barracks housed six foot soldiers, six mounted soldiers and their horses to boot. I did wonder where the soldiers who measured only 5'11" were housed!

We opted to have a meal at the 'oldest continually' as it was so full of history. Unfortunately the historical ambience was soon shattered by the television volume, so as soon as we had finished our meal, we headed back to Winnie and had an early night.

Soon after leaving Port Fairy the next morning, we found ourselves driving through an avenue of grey saltbush, with black crows on top of white posts and the splatter of grey and red of the road kill the only colour to break the bleakness. If you look at this section of the road on the map, it appears you will be travelling right next to the coast. But a continuous line of sand dunes hides the water, and trees misshapen through strong winds overhang the road at odd angles. I was more fascinated with the isolated tin shacks which are dotted at intervals along the edge of the salt lake. You hear of people wanting to opt out of society, and some days I can relate to this, but they also invariably choose a solitary existence. Why then, was it necessary to put several 'Children Crossing' signs along the road near these shacks? Soon this bleak landscape was changing and as we drove through an avenue of tall pine trees, we knew we were in the heart of the timber industry in the south-east of South Australia.

Our next overnight stop in Mt Gambier wasn't planned so we could feed the possums at dusk at the Umpherston Sinkhole, gaze upon the brilliant blue of the lake and climb down into the Cave Gardens with a picnic. Our motivation was purely sentimental, as this was the place we eloped to several years ago, and it happened to be our wedding anniversary the next day!

The weekend we were married was originally planned as a couple of days away to catch up with our friends from Melbourne, Lyn and Alan. Neither couple could be bothered driving the long distance between capital cities, so Mt Gambier seemed a good compromise.

But a few weeks before we were due to head off, Hon turned the sound down on *A Current Affair* and glanced in my direction. 'You know, if we were ever going to get married, this'd be the weekend to do it.'

Yes, I know what you're thinking – what a romantic fool! I was just about to tell him to get up off his knees – then realised he wasn't. I had already gone through the 'tulle and tantrums' many years ago, so another big wedding was the last thing I needed. Hon and I had bought a place together some years earlier, and were quite happy cohabiting 'sans certificate'. But after discussing it that night, we realised this was something we both wanted.

'We'd even have the witnesses,' he said, dangling the carrot even further.

Lyn is the same friend who accompanied me on that teenage week in Bright, enduring the car trip from hell with my pukin' poodle, and we had remained steadfast friends over the years. Al was her boyfriend even back then, so I could think of no other people I'd want more as witnesses at our wedding.

Our initial plan was to keep the wedding secret from our friends. We would just turn up and surprise them with the news on the day it was to happen. But then the 'girl' thing kicked in. Lyn would want to pack the right clothes, and would possibly murder me if she had to attend the ceremony in jeans and a t-shirt. A phone call to Melbourne that week started the tangled web I was about to weave.

'We thought we'd take you out to this posh restaurant on the Saturday night, so pack something dressy. The men are expected to wear a tie.'

A phone call from Lyn two days later was not the optimistic response I had hoped for. 'Al's complaining about having to wear a tie – he said it's supposed to be a weekend away, and that's where he wants to put the tie. But don't worry, Clairabelle, I'm packing my new black pants and top, so at least we girls will be dressed appropriately.'

No, this wasn't working. I could picture the wedding day scenario. Lyn hyperventilating as she stood there in her swish black outfit next to Al in his favourite fishing jumper and cords. So the next phone call, I told them our secret and they were both thrilled. We girls agreed that half the fun was the excitement of anticipation, and they certainly proved to be the perfect choice.

It was the happiest weekend and the preparation was certainly not without humour. The prospective 'gride and broom' arrived in Mt Gambier the day before the ceremony, just to finalise a few details. The outfit I had chosen was a long dress and matching jacket with simplicity the key. But as we took a stroll down the main street, I knew that to feel like a bride, I had to have flowers. Stepping into a hairdressing salon, I explained about the wedding and asked where the closest florist was. The woman, holding a comb in one hand, and a square of foil in the other, circled the counter and leaned towards my left shoulder. 'Gloria down at Coles does a laaarvlee arrangement,' she announced, sotto voce.

And when we walked through checkout number five the next day holding four long-stemmed roses and two buttonholes, not only did we agree it was 'laaarvlee' but also 'cheap at 'alf the price'.

In order to legalise the proceedings, we had to organise a Justice of the Peace. Fortunately the Mt Gambier Council proved helpful in this regard, and furnished us with an up-to-date list of the JPs in the area. As Hon and I were fans of a situation comedy set around the lives of three priests living together on a remote Irish island, we decided we couldn't go past a gentleman by the name of Edward.

'Father Ted,' we both said in unison, as our finger hit the name at the same time.

He sounded delightful on the phone, and when we called in to his place the night before the wedding to finalise details, he was more than welcoming. 'Please, sit down. I'm just going to put the kettle on, Joan's made a lovely fruit cake and she'd never forgive me if I didn't offer you a bit,' he said, as he disappeared through the door. 'Oh, Joan's in hospital, by the way,' he said, his head reappearing. 'Nothing serious, but she'll be sorry she's missed you. Now – that cup of tea – let me go and get it started.'

As we sat there listening to cups and saucers being rattled and a whistling kettle and a louder whistling host, we smiled at the numerous wedding photos on the mantelpiece. There must have been more than thirty smiling couples of varying age groups.

'Ted and Joan have either bred prolifically, or we're going to be joining that lot after tomorrow,' Hon commented.

We spent a wonderful hour with our 'nuptials director'. There were some formalities to be taken care of, and poor Ted nearly had a nervous conniption when I misunderstood him and signed one of the papers there and then.

'Oh dear - that needs to be signed on the day – er – let me see – I tell you what – no one need know. You just mime signing it tomorrow.'

When I hear of the traumas many people go through with their wedding, I'm tempted to suggest they head to Mt Gambier and knock on Ted's door.

Our last overnight stop was Beachport, two hundred and fifty-five kilometres away, and I dragged out the relevant brochure from the old brown bag.

'Bet you thought Beachport was named because it was close to the sea.'

'Sounds logical,' said Driver Dan.

'Nup, the Booandik Aborigines called it Wirmalngrang and the first European in the area, Nicholas Baudin, called it Rivoli, after some duke.'

'And...?'

'What?'

'Why was it called Beachport, then?'

'Don't know – that's all the brochure says. Beachport was not named because of its proximity to the sea. That's it!'

I did breathe a quick sigh of relief that we weren't heading for Wirmalngrang, however. If I could get Armidale and Armitage mixed up, it didn't take much to imagine what I'd do with 'Worm-gang'.

We stared out of our respective windows realising we had reached information overload. How do people head off and play tourists for months and sometimes years? I guess they reach a point where they couldn't give a toss about how a place came into being. They just find a pleasant spot, park the van and get on with doing, well, pretty much nothing at all.

Beachport turned out to be another very appealing town on the Limestone Coast, and as we were not too far away from Adelaide now, we would keep this one in mind for a future weekend getaway.

I love the way each small town has its own claim to fame, and Beachport is no exception. The town jetty measures 772 metres, and is one of the longest in Australia. The original plan was to build it nearly 1,300 metres long, but I suspect they were happy to settle for 'one of the' instead of 'the'.

Although we had some food in the 'bago kitchen – enough for a three course meal for twelve people, in fact! – I felt it would be a shame not to have experienced a meal at Beachport's original hotel.

The small two-storey building houses Bompa's by the Sea, which not only has an intimate bar, a café and the main restaurant, but guest rooms as well. People said the food was 'magnificent' and we found this statement irresistible. (Well, it was actually one 'people' – the shop owner up the road – and from the effusive accolades she gave the place, I suspected her son and daughter-in-law may have had the licence).

Our table afforded wonderful views of not only the foreshore but the famous 'one of the' jetty as well, and we were quite happy to sip up the atmosphere along with our pre-dinner drinks. But suddenly, what must have been the entire female population of Beachport and surrounding townships burst through the restaurant door. We watched as they surrounded the bar to commence their big night out.

'Jill, what are you drinking – want to go halves in a bottle of Riesling?'

'No, bugger it, I'm getting a whole bottle to myself, seeing Jan's driving.'

'Sue, are you still on Jammie and Coke?'

'Yeah, course, but make it Diet Coke. Had to lie down to get my zip up tonight!'

'No, I'll buy this one and you can get the next – oh, shit – bloody Ben's been in my purse again. I'll kill him!'

Oh, yes, I'd heard it all before. I've been on enough girls' nights to recognise the familiar patter.

'What's their story?' Hon asked when he saw me studying the group.

This was a game we often played when dining out, and filled in the time between placing our orders and waiting for the food to arrive. It started when we were holidaying in Queensland some years ago and were dining at a five-star hotel. At the table diagonally opposite was a group of Japanese, comprising six women and one man. We had been fascinated to watch the animated conversation of the women, whilst the man sat quietly concentrating on his meal.

As the waiter placed our meals in front of us, Hon looked at me. 'I wonder what the story is with that group. You'd think the guy would be happy, the only bloke travelling with six females. '

I had been thinking the same thing, but had already worked out a story to fit the scene. 'Their husbands all work for a large multinational firm in Tokyo that conducts courses to keep the wives of employees busy. These women attend a weekly origami class, and over the last few months, have all voiced an interest in travel. But unfortunately the husbands are too busy to take time off. When the wives approached their husbands about the women going on a trip as a group, the men agreed, providing their wives found a male chaperone. When one of the women produced her gay nephew, this seemed the ideal answer. And so the trip was planned! At first, the nephew was really excited about the offer of a free trip to Australia. All he needed to do was to book a few day tours and supervise the women's luggage, but now it was three weeks into the tour, and he was missing his boyfriend back home.'

Hon liked this story, and even though we often played this game, this was still his favourite scenario. But back at Bompa's, I was struggling to put a story together about the gaggle of girlfriends. My first thought was an office party, but as several of the women would be lucky to see seventy again, this wasn't really an option. And the thing that was really throwing me was their rather odd taste in clothes.

'No, it's no good. I want to know the real story this time. Be back in a tick,' I said, as I headed for the giggling group.

Five minutes later, I sat down at our table. 'It's a hens' night – that little one on the left is the bride – and the invitation read "Come dressed as the mother of the bride".'

There was a pause as we stared at each other, and then burst out laughing.

'I think it's pretty safe to say the bride's mother isn't in that lot. Either that or she has a brilliant sense of humour and a forgiving nature,' I said.

The girls under twenty-five years of age were the ones I couldn't take my eyes off. If they hadn't found a moth-eaten grey wig to wear, they had liberally sprinkled their hair with baby powder to give the same effect. Some had even drawn heavy wrinkles around the eyes and mouth and their choice of clothes ranged from tired-looking fox wraps, lace or silk dresses many adorned with marquesite brooches and finished the whole look off with tapestry or Oroton handbags. (But not the Oroton that has made a resurgence of late!)

'They look more like great grandmother of the bride,' I said, just a tad miffed. I was officially old enough to qualify as a mother of (the groom, in my case), and I took umbrage – and everything else – at their interpretation of our age group. And yet when I was their age, I couldn't understand why anyone would want to even live after the age of forty!

The food at Bompa's was great – 'magnificent' was stretching it – and well worth a return visit when our next weekend getaway came due. And we found another reason to revisit the area.

'Listen to this,' I said. 'There's a place called the Pool of Siloam. It's fed by underground springs and has seven times the salinity of the Dead Sea. If you're a non-swimmer you float, and you can even lie on your back and read a book.'

31

On the home stretch! We joined the south-eastern freeway just outside Murray Bridge, and it's only seventy-five kilometres to Adelaide. This freeway affords such a smooth ride and, as it's a road I have travelled several times before, I leant back, closed my eyes and reviewed the past few weeks. We had seen parts of Australia we had only read about, met fascinating people and covered thousands of kilometres in a caravan on steroids. But we had only really skimmed the surface of the places we visited, and there were so many spots we knew would be worth a return visit.

'Home at last!'

Hon's voice brought me back to the present, as we turned into our street. Why does everything in your neighbourhood feel and look different when you've been away? The street looked narrow and the houses unfamiliar, but then we turned into our driveway, and it all felt right.

As soon as Hon parked the 'bago– this time avoiding the eaves – I leapt out, slipped the key into the back door, and rushed inside. Our home smelt clean and fresh, thanks to our HFH (House-sitter From Heaven), but that was only a peripheral thought. I scanned the downstairs area looking for what I felt sure would be one bereft Burmese. Suddenly there was a slight movement on the couch, as a sleek black shape slowly stretched.

'Mummy's home – how's my beautiful boy?' I said.

Two yellow eyes with thin black slits appraised me, and I had to admit he was doing a sterling job of controlling his enthusiasm. I received a text message from the house-sitter three days into our journey, indicating Lord Poobah was unsure about the revised living arrangements. On the first morning after our departure, he had positioned himself in a central location, in order to monitor the comings and goings of the new landlady, at the same time managing to ignore any pathetic gestures of affection. This worried me at the time, but I didn't think the suggestion of returning home and bringing him back with us would have been at all popular – with either cat or husband. So I was more than relieved to receive a second text message two days later.

> Havn lie in this am wth Jordie curld nxt 2 me he luvs havn cuddles hope u r havn gr8 time dont wori bout n e thng xxx

At the time, this was the best news I could hear. There was no way I was going to enjoy my holiday if our boy was pining for us. But now I was getting a completely different perspective of the whole situation. He had not only adjusted to this new landlady, but decided to take us out of his memory banks altogether! Cupboard love – how shallow!

It took one hour, twenty-two minutes and thirteen seconds before he came round and realised we were his favourite people. Not that I was worried – no, really – and I'm confident all traces of HFH are erased from his brain – until we go away again, of course.

After we wandered through the house familiarising ourselves with everything again, we then had to face the unenviable task of emptying an entire mobile home, washing every piece of clothing – by this stage we couldn't remember what was dirty and what was clean – and finding places for all the souvenirs (or The Crap, as Hon called them). Out came the cardboard boxes to transport our gear from the Winnebago to the house, but there was little sign of the military precision followed when we were packing.

The last couple of weeks we had adopted a rather laissez-faire attitude to the inside of our house on wheels, so we were not too surprised to find packets of pasta in the shoe cupboard, souvenir fridge magnets amongst the dirty laundry and a packet of cereal in the bathroom cabinet (don't ask!). After countless journeys to and fro, the family room floor was starting to resemble a demolition site, as things were unceremoniously dumped wherever there was space. But by the end of the day everything had been unpacked, and we had cleaned and polished not only the inside of the Winnebago, but the outside as well. The final Winnie the Poo Ceremony had been performed, and let's just say I wouldn't have been surprised to receive the next water rates on A3-size paper.

Now it was time to catch up with family and friends.

On our travels we encountered many retired people who had bought a caravan, rented out their house (or even sold it in some cases) hugged the grandkids, and headed off into the sunset. There was no timeline; no 'let's give it six months and see how we go'. They were quite happy to embrace a nomadic existence, and some admitted that whilst they would pop back home every now and again, being on the road was the life they preferred.

Then there were the baby boomers! I had my own theory on what motivated them to hit the road. They were all trying to avoid their adult children who were refusing to move out of the family home, even though the children were about to reach the double birthday numbers that start with three.

'Mum, how come there's absolutely nothing to eat in this house? How could you take ten dollars a fortnight from me and not supply stuff I like?'

'But Dad, that's my investment property. Hello! I get rent from it. You honestly don't expect me to live there, surely!'

'Oh God, Mother, how can I be expected to do my own ironing when I have to go out to work?'

Yes, they all had the same look, these boomers – they were running away. Either that or they were part of the witness protection program, but surely not in such great numbers! But didn't they miss their friends? I couldn't wait to catch up with ours, and when we did, the question was always the same.

'How was your trip? Would you hire a motorhome again?'

The first few times I was asked, I wasn't too sure how to respond. There was no doubt in my mind that I loved rambling around the countryside, and the whole experience was something I'll remember for years to come. But would I do it in a motorhome again?

Let's see – well, on the one hand, there is the... But then again I wasn't too fond of... But hey, that bit did end up being quite funny. Hang on, I think it's time for one of my lists. This one is called the AO list – the Advantages Of. Let's look at the advantages of staying in motels.

Arrival: open door, walk inside, dump suitcase and fix drink – beautiful!

Toilet facilities: your responsibility ends after you push the button. You don't care where it goes or even where it ends up. You're sure the contents of the pan will break down and this is far preferable than the same thing happening to you!

Bed and bathroom linen: stay in the right motel and this gets changed daily. And I must say I'm rather fond of the fan designs the staff create from a piece of towelling and leave displayed on the end of your bed.

Catering facilities: there are just three words you need to read on the motel information sheet – 'Room Service Available'. And if you prefer something else other than a club sandwich, every hotel has a more than adequate dining room.

Departure: leave bed unmade, zip up suitcase, walk out and close door – beautiful!

Sounding pretty good so far, wouldn't you agree? But in all fairness, we have to do a comparison. So I present you with the PG list – Probable Glitches you may encounter with your motorhome.

Arrival: you're so exhausted from lowering steps, connecting electricity, switching the fridge to gas, putting the cover up on the stove and turning the water pump on, you haven't got the energy to pour yourself a well deserved drink.

Toilet facilities: I think I've said it all!

Bed and bathroom linen: you realise you've only packed one set of sheets and find yourself in the caravan park laundromat at eleven-thirty p.m. reading about the impending nuptials of Prince Charles and Lady Diana Spencer.

Catering facilities: you too will fall in love with the cute little sink and the dinky little stove and the more than adequate storage area for your food. But soon after heading off (probably the second day) one thing becomes clear – ONLY AN IDIOT TAKES HER KITCHEN ON HOLIDAYS!

Departure: if you don't make sure the steps are up, the cupboard doors have been secure, the water pump is turned off, the fridge is switched back to gas, et cetera, bloody et cetera, something dire will happen and your holiday home will become a dangerous hellhole on wheels!

I do hope I haven't shattered anyone's dreams. Everyone's experience is going to be different, and if you want to do your own Winnebago Wander or Britz Blitz, you're not going to be put off. And it is one hell of an experience, no matter how you look at it.

But one final thing – and this is for my mother, if she can hear me up there. You were wrong, Mum. Road travel does agree with me. And you know what else I discovered? It is possible to travel around the countryside without a roll of toilet paper in your glovebox!

www.ingramcontent.com/pod-product-compliance
Lightning Source LLC
Chambersburg PA
CBHW030908080526
44589CB00010B/201